Rethinking ASIA

Entrepreneurship and Economic Development

Rethinking Asia
Entrepreneurship and Economic Development

Second Edition May 2, 2017
Copyright © 2017 by Center for Asia Leadership Initiatives
Printed in Seoul, Korea

A Publication of the Center for Asia Leadership Initiatives
Acumen Publishing
14 Nancy Lane Waltham MA 02452 USA

Center for Asia Leadership Initiatives
Website: www.asialeadership.org
Facebook: www.facebook.com/asiagroup

Asia Leadership Trek
Website: www.asialeadershiptrek.org
Facebook: www.facebook.com/asialeadershiptrek
Twitter & Weibo: @Asia_Trek

Library of Congress Control Number 2017938910
KDP ISBN: 979-8-3407944-7-5
US $13.99

For inquiries on partnership or sponsorship, or purchase of the publication, please email us at: cali@asialeadership.org

Entrepreneurship and
Economic Development

*Essays by Harvard, MIT, Tufts, and Stanford University students
who journeyed through 18 cities in 10 countries in Asia*

RETHINKING ASIA

2

Hungsoo S. Kim & Ursula DeYoung

2rd Edition

ACUMEN™
PUBLISHING

To all the aspiring leaders of this world

| Table of Contents |

•••

Introduction

Part 1 • Asia Leadership Trek

| About the Editors |

•••

Hungsoo S. Kim, a Korean national, is the Co-founder and President of the Center for Asia Leadership Initiatives. Passionate about nurturing and empowering talents in Asia, he has been actively engaging various stakeholders in developing and running over twenty-five programs in more than twenty-two countries in Asia to help emerging leaders explore opportunities to be socially responsible in facing the region's complex challenges. These programs fall under the Center's four main initiatives, namely the Asia Leadership Trek, a public diplomacy arm for scholars at Harvard, Stanford, MIT, and Fletcher; the Asia Leadership Institute, a leadership capacity-building arm; the Acumen Case Center, a research and content development arm; and Acumen Publishing, a publication arm. Hungsoo oversees these initiatives, along with a team of twenty comprising Faculty and Teaching Fellows from Harvard and Stanford University, and administrators at the main office in Boston, U.S., and the Asian regional headquarters in Kuala Lumpur, Malaysia.

As part of his continuous endeavor toward grooming leaders of tomorrow, Hungsoo recently joined the Asia Future Institute, a Seoul-based policy and leadership think tank, as Executive Director to instill in Korean and Northeast Asian talents the drive and passion to create positive social change through effective leadership. He prides himself on accelerating efforts to reach out to all forty-eight countries in Asia by 2022. Hungsoo's areas of research and training, among others, include 'Negotiation and Mediation,' 'Adaptive Leadership,' 'Persuasion and Influence,' and 'Creative Confidence.' To date, some twenty-five thousand burgeoning and established leaders from the government, non-profits, and corporate world in Asia have benefited from these programs.

Prior to establishing the Center, Hungsoo worked for twelve years in varying sectors from strategy consulting and social entrepreneurship to international development, politics, and government. He has also served as a policy aide in the United Nations in New York representing Korea, and as a project analyst at UNESCO in Paris. He currently sits on the board of two non-profit organizations, and has served as a visiting scholar at the Asia Center at Harvard University and at the Kellogg School of Management in Northwestern University. Hungsoo holds a Masters of Public Administration from the Harvard Kennedy School of Government; Masters in International Cooperation from the Graduate School of International Studies, Seoul National University; and completed his undergraduate studies with two majors in U.S. and International Law, and International Politics with a minor in Economics from Handong University.

Ursula DeYoung is a novelist and editor living in Cambridge, MA. She received her BA from Harvard in 2004 and her Ph.D. in History from Oxford in 2009. Her first non-fiction book, published in 2011, was a biographical study of 19th century physicist, John Tyndall. Her first novel, Shorecliff, was published by Little, Brown in 2013.

| About the Contributors |

•••

Vivian Yuhang Wang, from Jilin, China, received her MBA from Harvard Business School in 2015. She earned her B.A. *magna cum laude* in Economics from Princeton University. After Princeton she joined Credit Suisse as an investment banking analyst at the Strategic Finance Group, advising the firm's global clients on their corporate finance and risk-management decisions. Vivian later became the first investment analyst at Teng Yue Partners, a New York-based investment-management firm, where she conducted extensive research on public companies in various industries in China. At both Teng Yue Partners and Harvard Business School, Vivian expanded her passion for global investments across different asset classes while deepening her understanding of fundamental equity investments, macroeconomics, and international relations. Her evolving perspectives in economics and finance, as well as her interest in Asia, have driven Vivian to pursue research in these fields both academically and professionally.

Alanna Hughes obtained a Master's degree in Public Administration (MPA) from Harvard Kennedy School and a Master's degree in Business Administration (MBA) from MIT Sloan. Originally from the Boston area, Alanna launched the first Caribbean chapter of a social enterprise focused on microconsignment, worked on Ashoka's Full Economic Citizenship team in Washington, D.C., and served as a Community Economic Development Adviser with the Peace Corps in the Dominican Republic. Alanna is particularly interested in introducing new technologies and platforms into emerging economies, as well as strengthening the entrepreneurial ecosystems of these markets. She has worked as Head of Sales for an ecommerce startup in Angola and done research as an "Innovation Diplomat" for MIT's Regional Entrepreneurship Acceleration Program (REAP). Alanna holds a B.S.F.S. from Georgetown University's

Walsh School of Foreign Service. She enjoys learning new languages, traveling, exploring open-air markets, dancing, and doing virtually anything involving the ocean.

Greg Manne, from Ft. Lauderdale, Florida, received his Master's in Higher Education at the Harvard Graduate School of Education. As an undergraduate at Boston College, Greg developed a passion for education, majoring in Secondary Education and History. After graduation he was awarded a Fulbright Teaching Fellowship and moved to Madrid, Spain. During his time in Madrid, Greg taught a variety of subjects to high school students at IES Isaac Albéniz, including civics, history, music, and English. He expanded his focus to higher education by working as a research assistant and study-abroad coordinator at Complutense University. Greg was also selected as an inaugural member of the U.S. Embassy Youth Council Program in Spain, where he helped to facilitate programs related to volunteering, education, and cultural exchange for college students and young adults. Currently, Greg works as the Special Assistant to the Dean of Admissions at Tufts University and as a Teaching Fellow at the Harvard Graduate School of Education.

Parul Batra is an MBA candidate at the MIT Sloan School of Management. She is passionate about using technology and design thinking to solve challenging development problems and has a special interest in education and employment innovation. Her educational and professional background spans technology, business, and policy. She is originally from New Delhi, India, and received her Bachelor's degree in Computer Science from Delhi University. Prior to business school, she worked on HIV financing in Sub-Saharan Africa at the Clinton Health Access Initiative (CHAI) and in management consulting at McKinsey & Company. More recently, she has worked on bridging the education-to-employment gap in Kenya and the US and as a Product Manager at Prism, a retail analytics start-up based in San Francisco.

Bryant Renaud grew up in the Maryland suburbs of Washington, D.C. As an undergraduate at Williams College, he spent his time learning how economic policy interacts with public health and pandemics. After college, Bryant worked with governments around the world, ranging from Thailand to Ethiopia, on economic policy promoting pro-poor, inclusive growth. At the Brookings Institution, Bryant researched health and fiscal policy. After working with the Oregon governor's director of natural resources on wildfire suppression, Bryant partnered with several Boston-area municipalities, including Chelsea, Fitchburg, and Lawrence, to help them make better use of their data resources and provide better services. Now studying for a Master's in Public Policy at the Harvard Kennedy School, he is continuing to focus on economic policy, with a particular emphasis on energy and infrastructure. As a member of the Winter 2015 ALT, Bryant was struck by the social, cultural, and economic strings that bind us all together, and he was touched by the welcome he received at every stop of the journey.

Rachel Mason, as a *summa cum laude* graduate of the Human Development and Psychology Master's Program at the Harvard Graduate School of Education, Rachel is passionate about optimizing the well-being of others in individual, organizational, and educational contexts. Rachel grew up in Richmond, VA, and earned her undergraduate degree at Virginia Commonwealth University. Throughout her life, she has faced the challenge of navigating the conventionally perceived duality of her biracial identity; her consequent ability to trace and develop the connections within her diverse family has translated into a global understanding of human connectedness. After teaching English to adolescents in China, Rachel entered a Ph.D. program in Clinical Psychology in the Fall of 2016. Her research interests focus on the intersection of clinical psychology with the mind-body-spirituality relationship.

Evelyn Peiqi Ooi Widjaja is a research associate at the Institute of Southeast Asian Studies / Yusof Ishak Institute in Singapore. She holds a Bachelor of Science in Economics from Singapore Management University and a Master's of Education in International Education Policy. She is keenly interested in public policy and in issues that contribute to the growth of countries and youth development. Her career spans both the public and private sectors, where she conducts independent research work and assists post-doctorate fellows in their work. She seeks to make an impact on society in whatever work she does.

Jaye Buchbinder served as the Design Thinking Fellow on the Summer 2015 Asia Leadership Trek, leading both design thinking workshops and problemanalysis exercises, in which students learned to apply these innovative thinking skills to real-world issues. Originally from Long Beach, California, Jaye completed her undergraduate degree in S tainable Design and Engineering at Stanford and is currently working on her Master's degree there in Management Science and Engineering, combining the quantitative skills of optimization and probabilistic analysis with more qualitative design thinking and management skills.

Eugene B. Kogan, is Director of the American Secretaries of State Project: Diplomacy, Negotiations and Statecraft, a joint initiative of the Future of Diplomacy Project at Harvard Kennedy School, the Program on Negotiation at Harvard Law School, and Harvard Business School. Dr. Kogan leads the American Secretaries of State Project's research and administrative efforts as the new Project prepares to interview all former U.S. Secretaries of State about the most demanding and consequential negotiations they conducted while serving in the nation's highest foreign policy office. Dr. Kogan is a former Stanton Nuclear Security Postdoctoral Fellow at the Belfer Center for Science and International Affairs at Harvard Kennedy School. He specializes in coercive negotiations and holds a Ph.D. in Politics from Brandeis University. Dr. Kogan is working on a book on nuclear negotiations based on his doctoral thesis, which was awarded Harvard Law School Program on Negotiation's 2014 Raiffa Award for the Best Student Doctoral Paper. He has previously co-taught a course on military instruments of foreign policy at Harvard Extension School.

John Lim, is Co-founder and Managing Director of CALI Boston. A former fellow of the Harvard University Asia Center, he has worked in diverse organizations including the Embassy of Canada in Korea, the International Crisis Group, and in different sectors such as English education and social entrepreneurship. His current work engages him in researching and applying various leadership, education, and entrepreneurial models and frameworks within the Asian contexts.

| Foreword |

•••

The growing interest in both the opportunities and the challenges in Asia is unsurprising, considering how much economic and political growth Asia has seen over the last decade. While numerous books have analyzed the quantitative data on these developments, this book offers something different: an immersive experience that strips away the numbers and narrates the journey of young leaders from the other side of the globe (or Trekkers), on a study trip covering several Asian countries. They meet senior political leaders, high-ranked businessmen, and a cross-section of local citizens, interspersing these meetings with visits to historical and cultural sites. The combination of these experiences allows for an in-depth exploration of the underlying trends and future direction of these countries and their peoples, and the results are encapsulated in the following chapters.

Hungsoo S. Kim, a research scholar at the Asia Center, is the organizing mind behind this program. Already he has put together several groups of scholars from Harvard, MIT, and Stanford for educational trips across Asia. Coming from numerous different countries and backgrounds including management consulting, finance, academia, and government, the Trekkers on each trip exchange ideas with Asian leaders on such topics as entrepreneurship, education, and leadership. They learn to see things from multiple perspectives, as individuals from specific cultures and as global citizens. During the course of their trips they see through the eyes of educators, policymakers, officials, and entrepreneurs.

In 2015, this intense and holistic exposure was experienced by two different groups of Trekkers – first on the ALT 2015 Trek in January, which covered Japan, China, Korea, Indonesia, Malaysia, India and Nepal, and second on the ALT V Trek in June, which covered the Philippines, China, Hong Kong, Thailand, Korea and Mongolia. Accounts from both Treks are presented in this book.

In each chapter, a Trekker offers his or her unique perspective on a particular aspect of today's Asia, whether it be a comparative study of Asian macroeconomics or a detailed analysis of Indonesia's start-up scene. All the chapters relate to the themes of entrepreneurship and economic development in Asia, topics that impinge on every aspect of life – political, social, educational, cultural – in the Asian countries visited on the Treks.

Many of the Trekkers who go on these astonishing trips later move on to internships or permanent positions in Asia, in order to explore specific localities in greater depth and to cement their connections within a particular Asian country. Such bonds exemplify the goal of the Asia Leadership Trek Program, which is the beneficial exchange of knowledge, outlooks, and ideas.

This book is sui generis. It follows the extraordinary path of handpicked candidates from some of the finest universities in the world, allowing readers to explore Asia as if they themselves were there with the intrepid Trekkers.

Enjoy the journey!

Arthur Kleinman
Victor and William Fung Director
Harvard University Asia Center

Introduction

| Introduction |

Setting the Asia Leadership Trek in Context

Hungsoo S. Kim, Co-Editor
MPA, Harvard Kennedy School of Government

● ● ●

High-rise condominiums, a gigantic resort, and a lagoon-themed park formed the view from my office in the Sunway Graduate Center—a reminder that I was halfway across the world from Boston. A total of three years—one and a half at the Harvard Kennedy School of Government (HKS) and one and a half beyond its walls, in Asia—led to the establishment of the Center for Asia Leadership Initiatives (CALI) in Kuala Lumpur, Malaysia, the regional headquarters of CALI in Boston and currently houses many programs, including the Asia Leadership Trek.

Prior to these three years, I enjoyed a stable career with a promising future, as well as a lovely, expanding family. Studying at the Kennedy School was an incredible privilege, yet it also brought many challenges, given the consequent lack of a steady income and the need for me to support and spend time with my adorable little children. Thankfully, eschewing a lucrative but unimaginative career in favor of a degree in Public Administration drove me to search for deeper, more tangible ways to put my time in Boston to good use. I reached out to my professors to discuss what I had learned through my course materials and made close friends who shared my visions of an educational program embracing the diversity of Asia. My cohort at the HKS represented nearly every corner of the earth. Their experiences were varied, with both successes and failures, and their wisdom and strength inspired me to hope that social change can indeed happen in a meaningful way.

Galvanized and equipped by my time at the HKS, I quickly established a footprint in Asia. What started off as a one-country Trek with a handful of Trekkers has now blossomed into eight Treks with a total of about three hundred twenty Trekkers, representing thirty-nine countries. We even organized a special Mongolia Trek, one of the few remaining countries on our unvisited list, to round off an impressive array of seventeen countries and thirty-nine cities. To date, we have chalked up approximately one hundred thirty-five thousand miles of intra-regional travel. I am very proud of the Asia Leadership Trek, its organizing team, and especially the Trekkers themselves, for achieving so much in such a short period of time. The remaining figures are a further testimony to their achievement:

Conferences Organized	Meetings and Site-Visits
49 conferences	5 Heads of State
8,800 Participants	47 Ministers or equivalent
Given 47 Workshop Topics	154 Companies
Given 38 TED-style Talks	27 Foundations
	24 Educational Institutions
	62 Non-profit Organizations
	21 International Organizations

The birth of the ALT was sparked by the hope of connecting the vast educational resources at the Harvard Kennedy School with individuals and organizations in Asia who are working to address the core challenges of the 21st century. The ALT's core mission is to assist and empower individuals, organizations, and governmental bodies to play a more active and meaningful leadership role in their communities, through learning and service. It is a mission that applies to everyone involved, from the students coming from Harvard, MIT, Tufts, and Stanford to the leaders, citizens, and organizations we engage with in Asia.

The ALT operates under the framework of "Head, Hands, and Heart," or "Knowing, Doing and Being." In brief, this philosophy encourages people to acquire a practical understanding of our world and the best practices that drive progress and change; to put into practice what we know in order to contribute to our communities; and to understand who we are and what our roles and responsibilities are in improving the world for ourselves and others. To accomplish these aims, the ALT offers socioeconomic, political, and cultural study trips, combined with public-service opportunities, in multiple cities across Asia. During our journeys, the ALT team, organizers and Trekkers alike, seek to apply and share the knowledge they have gained in their graduate courses, reinforced with their own personal experiences, through leadership conferences and workshops.

The Treks play a pivotal role in complementing the Trekkers' classroom learning at Harvard, MIT, Tufts, and Stanford by giving them access to key leaders and decision-makers in Asia, presenting them with direct and multiple perspectives on the challenges and opportunities that Asian societies face today, and giving them the opportunity to teach what they have learned to others. Each Trek thus offers in-depth experiential learning, in which theories and ideas turn into real-life events and interactions. The Treks also allow their participants to engage with regular citizens; in every journey, the Trekkers learn an immense amount from the people they meet, while at the same time offering hope, knowledge, and inspiration through mentorship, stories about leadership, discussions of best practices, and capacity-building workshops on such topics as leadership, innovation and entrepreneurship.

The Trekkers also learn from each other. When you draw together participants from many different institutions—Harvard's Kennedy School, School of Education, and Business School, MIT's Sloan School of Management, and Tufts' Fletcher School of Law and Diplomacy, among others—you can expect a spirited exchange. In the semester before they travel to Asia, the Trekkers design workshops, write speeches, and share their thoughts about the trip ahead. Community sessions and working-group meetings help to foster a collegial and convivial environment, in which the students can get to know each other in both formal and informal settings, and these bonds are strengthened further on the Trek itself, with constant interactions ranging from conversations at the breakfast table to long discussions on the journeys between destinations.

●●●

In the past few years, the ALT has inspired several additional institutions: among them the Asia Leadership Institute, which builds leadership capacity in youths, scholars, and working professionals in

Asia; the Acumen Case Center, which offers programs and contents that address the transmission-heavy, rote-based model of education prevalent in many classrooms in Asia; and Acumen Publishing, which offers related research, development, and publications. All of these institutions strive to educate and support capable and ethical leaders, to help organizations play leadership roles in their communities, to disseminate world-leading practices and instructive tools, and to create platforms and events for the exchange of ideas and expertise. The Asia Leadership Institute, Acumen Case Center and Acumen Publishing are already up and running, while the Asia Innovation Lab is in development stage. We also plan to develop online learning platforms for the eight thousand eight hundred alumni who have gone through our ALT and ALI programs, thus cementing the links we have made among countries all over the world through online connections.

In January of 2016, our eighth Trek will cover five countries: China—specifically Shanghai, a trend-setting metropolis and a role model for other cities in China because of its booming economy, financial restructuring, and modernization strategies; Singapore, a nation heading trends on many metrics while facing challenges related to diversity, population, and growth; Malaysia, which has the highest GDP per capita after Singapore in Southeast Asia but is mired by complicated racial issues and political challenges; Cambodia, a country offering valuable lessons in post-conflict peace-building while simultaneously tackling the problems of human rights and human trafficking; and, finally, Bangladesh, a country plagued by poverty, overpopulation, and environmental challenges that has nonetheless made significant strides, even being deemed a "Next Eleven" emerging economy.

Later in 2016 we will push the boundaries of our traditional Treks by hosting a Trek to Central Asia. This region is often neglected in discussions of Asia because of the strong focus on China and India, but given its bridging location between East and West, historically a key portion of the Silk Road, the region deserves close attention and analysis. Recently there has been a growing interest in the region from global scholars and increasing participation in world discussions by the region's many stakeholders. Furthermore, its countries, including Kazakhstan, Uzbekistan, and Tajikistan, are well-endowed with resources and culturally diverse, promising an enriching experience for the Trekkers.

Other new Treks in 2016 are the Asia Innovation Trek (AIT) held in March, and the Global Leadership Trek (GLT) organized in August. The AIT is designed to benefit policy-makers, corporate executives and educators in Asia, as they journey with distinguished participants from world-renowned schools to explore Asia's Silicon Valley. For this Trek, we sought applications from candidates beyond Harvard, MIT, Tufts, and Stanford, reaching out in particular to such universities as Yale, Columbia, and Princeton. We also included participants from the private, government, non-profit, and educational sectors, which considerably widened our pool of potential recruits and ensured that many more candidates, the best of the best from around the world, are given to chance to take part in the development of Asia.

To enhance the ALT's operational capabilities, we have hired eight new international and local staff-members to work in our Kuala Lumpur center, heading our new programs. Moreover, to increase both the quality and the quantity of our teaching programs, we collaborated with four faculty members from Harvard and twelve part-time Teaching Fellows from Harvard and Stanford University. Their contributions strengthened the ALT as well as CALI's many educational ventures.

I and the other leaders of the ALT are proud of the fact that the Trek, in both its philosophical framework and its practical execution, relies heavily on the resources and people of Harvard. In the future, we plan to seek similar partnerships with other schools and universities in complementary fields, such as the Stanford Graduate School of Business and Princeton Woodrow Wilson Center, in order to enhance our existing practices and thus better serve our Trekkers and, ultimately, Asian communities.

● ● ●

The Center for Asia Leadership (CALI Malaysia), our new regional headquarters in Kuala Lumpur, was established in collaboration with the Jeffrey Cheah Foundation (JCF). Before confirming our agreement with the JCF, we were honored to receive offers from three other countries: a foundation in Japan offered us a ten-year grant; Mongolia offered us a tract of land and a generous endowment; and a wealthy, philanthropic individual in Hong Kong offered us a sizeable grant.

In the end, we decided on Malaysia, signing an agreement with the JCF and the Sunway Education Group (SEG), for a number of reasons. Their staff have shown extraordinary enthusiasm and competence in their handling of key tasks and duties for our programs. From the first, their professionalism demonstrated their integrity and made it easy for both sides to trust and depend on each other. Our collaboration has also given us access to several valuable resources, including the facilities at SEG; logistical, human resources and legal departments that will help facilitate the transfer of our operations; and a proximity to other institutes in the neighborhood. CALI Malaysia has already benefited from the local network that the SEG has provided, and in return the SEG can take advantage of the international and regional network surrounding the CALI.

Our collaboration with the SEG is possible thanks to Dr. Jeffrey Cheah, the founding trustee of JCF and a man who shares our values of inspiring and improving society—among others, one of which is to cultivate his educational arm as the Asia's Harvard University. His foundation has given out over 23,000 scholarships to deserving students, valued over US $50 million. Such an achievement exemplifies Dr. Cheah's aims, which align with our own and form the basis of our partnership. It is one that I trust will continue for many years.

This book is a direct result of our collaboration. It offers nine thoughtful analyses of a range of Asian countries and issues, written by Trekkers whose reflections and perspectives stem from their own backgrounds, their observations, and their learning goals. As Asia poises itself to surge ahead, it is becoming more and more important to connect its talent base with the future leaders of other countries, so that both sides can benefit and so that the Trekkers, as they begin their leadership careers, can experience the power, resources, and potential of Asia. Based on both scholarly research and personal observations, this collection of essays demonstrates some of the ways in which this exchange of ideas has developed, focusing in particular on the ever-evolving subject of entrepreneurship and economic development in Asia. I hope you enjoy the read!

Part 1

·
·

Asia Leadership Trek

Chapter 1

Macroeconomics, Progress, and Asia

Vivian Yuhang Wang

MBA, Harvard Business School

● ● ●

Introduction

"Where are you going? The lecture is starting in minutes!" My friend turned to look at me as she walked into the classroom, her breath turning into soft white mist in the freezing air. "I'm going for a quick run!" I answered as I dashed outdoors and started a lap around the school building. I was not training for a junior marathon; I was simply trying to stay focused. In the long, dark winter days in my hometown in Northeast China, there was insufficient heating at my middle school, and without going for a quick run beforehand to generate some body heat, I would have been too cold to get through the hour-long lectures.

I have always considered myself very fortunate, for my path was filled with improvement. Back in those cold days, there was no such thing as a snow day. School hours were long and sometimes extended into the weekends. Every family was eager to give their only child the best education possible and insisted that he or she work hard. It did not matter that we had very little material wealth to enjoy. Our progress generated daily excitement and made us content. Even in harsh conditions, my classmates and I shared this drive, working hard because of a powerful hope that with more knowledge and better grades there would be a brighter future ahead of us.

Many years later, I arrived as a freshman on Princeton's beautiful campus, where lush greenery stood as a backdrop for the bright smiles of the incoming students. The university felt like a dreamland to me. Mesmerized by its incomprehensible abundance, both material and intellectual, I was shocked as much by the buffet-style dinners, where half of the food on each plate went straight to the waste bin, as by the notion that an undergraduate student could drop by during a professor's office hours and receive undivided attention. While feeling immensely grateful for the scholarship that enabled me to study there, I had to wrestle with a deep sense of uneasiness: how could so many of my American friends buy new shoes on credit every month, when my equally brilliant, hardworking peers in China spend endless hours of work while owning and consuming so much less?

With questions like these in mind, I majored in economics, eager to take full advantage of the world-class academic resources at Princeton. I dove into numbers, equations, charts, trends, regressions, simulations. My extensive mathematics and statistics preparation in China served me well, especially when I focused on quantitative economics. Yet, despite acing all of my economics classes, I felt unsatisfied with my learning: I was not tackling the fundamental questions. To my undergraduate self, real growth and inflation were just numbers; the luxury of credit and the burden of debt were only theoretical phenomena, existing solely in PowerPoint presentations. Though I could see the vast differences between my experiences in China and in America, I could not feel the pain or the joy for myself, nor did I question the origins of the theories I was learning. I simply studied and accepted them.

After graduation, I spent several years in investment banking and investment management in New York, gaining practical knowledge and earning a healthy income. But my desire to understand the deeper significance of economics did not lessen, and soon I returned to school. Now, pursuing an MBA at the Harvard Business School, I have many opportunities to ponder my unresolved questions. In my studies I attempt to apply the analytical tools I have acquired, in order to explain the stark economic differences between the developed and developing worlds. Years of learning in economics, finance, statistics, business, and politics are gradually coming together in my mind to form a picture of something I have always wanted to understand—how economics works in the real world.

Japan: A Quest for New Growth

Sitting on the high-speed train from Narita airport to downtown Tokyo, I glanced out the window to see miles of green fields and thousands of low-rise houses slowly transforming into tall buildings, crisscrossing power grids, colorful billboards, and bustling streets. I decided to join the Asia Leadership Trek (ALT), bringing my questions and curiosity to places geographically close to where I come from, but markedly different in many ways. I was excited to see Japan for the first time. To most other Asian countries, Japan is an enviable symbol of economic development; to my family and friends back home, Japan stands for exceptional order and unimaginable cleanness; to my professors in the U.S., who taught macroeconomics decades ago, Japan was the once miraculous rising superpower that elicited fancy and fear among the Western world but ultimately perplexed them with a surprising downturn. Here in Tokyo, I began to wonder what Japan means to her own people.

The following day, armed with a seven-page, gamified instruction booklet provided by a fellow Trekker, I set out on my own for the National Youth Olympic Center, via public transit. Standing with my luggage in front of the ticketing machine, I counted out the unfamiliar coins. With slight help from my recognition of Kanji, I pulled a subway ticket from the slot, just like the millions of locals who pass through Shinjuku station every day. Tokyo appeared to be an extremely well-oiled machine, fine-tuned to allow every part of it to perform at the highest accuracy and speed. Already, I began to feel grounded in this city.

This feeling of connection was reaffirmed when we were greeted by the Japanese students at the ALT conference the next day. During Ms. Santhi Suppiah's workshop on "Leading with Passion," the local participants eagerly and openly shared the challenges they faced at school and work, also expressing their aspirations to make positive changes. Primed with the goal of understanding Japan's current economic landscape and the views of its people, I compared their stories with what I had read about Abenomics, the economic policies advocated by Mr. Shinzo Abe, Prime Minister of Japan. Students and young business leaders desire more entrepreneurship, greater innovation, and higher expectations of prosperity; they are hungry for revitalization in their everyday life.

Yet, despite these high hopes, there seems to be a powerful force holding these young people back from fully unleashing their potential and creativity. Visitors soon discover that Japan is a society with the utmost respect for rules and—perhaps by extension—an unquestioned support of industrialism. As we found during our visit to the Shinto Shrine on New Year's Eve, there is a strong tradition in Japan of pursuing purity, peace, and sincerity, a tradition that operates without written doctrine but flows through every daily task. When we were touring around the city, we could see innumerable elements of these unspoken philosophies, from carefully painted lines for queuing outside a snack stand to families of three generations paying orderly visits to temples and shrines.

How can a culture, a people, a country that values diligence, attention to detail, talent, and technology suffer "two loss decades" in its economic progress? This question came into my mind again and again as I immersed myself in Tokyo's duality of tradition and modernism. How was each micro-unit of yen, loan, tool, man-hour, woman-hour used in this nation, and how did that use lead to such a different aggregate outcome from that of other countries? Was the downturn simply a result of the population's low expectations—a grand trickery of national psychology in which the economy declined simply because it was expected to decline? Or did these challenges arise as the outcome of past wars? Were they so deeply entrenched as to be insoluble, or would it be possible to redesign a system and an institution that would help rejuvenate this economy?

I was eager to find more clues as I listened to talks given by Professor Takenaka Harukata at the National Graduate Institute For Policy Studies. He argued that the very institutional design of Japan's political system and legislative process deters swift decision-making. Therefore, despite Prime Minister Abe's popularity and strong will, he will continue to find it challenging to push through reforms, especially on deeper issues addressing productivity as outlined in the "third arrow" of Abenomics. Historically Japan has shown a strong regulative response to economic pains. For instance, a special bill is now required for the Bank of Japan to issue bonds, thanks to memories of painful inflation caused by overheated prewar credit expansion. Adding to this complexity, Mr. Abe's shifted focus towards security policies has called the credibility and effectiveness of his economic policies into question. Despite overwhelming support from older voters, it remains debatable whether Mr. Abe can increase sufficient awareness and enlist enough participants to enact his economic reforms, especially among the younger population.

In his interactive and data-rich presentation on Abenomics, Mr. Hiroaki Kuwajima, Chief Financial Officer at Aoyama Shachu Corporation, offered another interpretation of the challenges that Japan faces in its pursuit of new growth. Despite soaring stock-market performances and improving unemployment figures in the past few years under Mr. Abe's policies, credit creation and exports remained sluggish, while real wages consistently declined. Japan continues to face an estimated 1 percent annual population decline, insufficient capital investment, and accelerated competition in global manufacturing, amidst increasing off-shoring activities.

From conversations that I had with students and entrepreneurs, it seems that the country's economy still suffers from a lot of red tape.

Inflexibility at the administrative level and labor restrictions hinder entrepreneurship and competition among small businesses. I would argue that the key question for Japan is this: to what degree can the state and monetary policies encourage competitiveness and productivity among private participants in the country's economy?

Strolling down a busy Tokyo street, I found myself in an engaging conversation with our student guide, Taka, on our walk towards Mori Tower for a night view of the dazzling Tokyo skyline. Though he had grown up in Tokyo, Taka had also studied in a high school exchange program in California, and he stood out from his peers both because he dressed differently and because he was much more comfortable conversing with us in English. In an authentic American accent, he told me that his friends in Japan are still either unaware of or uncomfortable with the need to develop the new skills and visions required for thriving in today's rapidly changing and ever more interconnected world. For them, Japan's politics are a game for parents and grandparents, and because of this reluctance to take part in their country's development, they run the risk of being trapped in a follower's mindset and destiny.

Surprised by his acute observations, I asked him about the controversial topic of history textbooks in Japan, which leave out many crucial facts about Japan's actions during World War II. "What did you learn about this issue in the U.S., and what do you think about it now?" I asked. He replied, "I was upset that we didn't get to learn more about it back home. We did a lot of bad things during the war, and I think young people in Japan should know about them." His answer was both humble and mature, and his poise reminded me of a Japanese international student in Boston who once said to me: "A lot of people in Japan confuse the acknowledgment of wrongdoings during the war with a lack of patriotism. I am proudly Japanese, and I love my country deeply. I don't think my patriotism is in conflict with knowing and teaching the tragedies of the war or with taking responsibility. If anything, that stance will make us stronger and allow us to improve as a nation."

After speaking with Taka, I felt a beam of hope for revived growth in his home country. I pondered the fact that despite its inflexibility in many areas, Japan also produces young people like Taka and my Boston friend, who are able to see insightfully and sensitively into their nation's ethos. The trait that I find most striking in both of them is their willingness to learn openly and think critically in drastically different environments. For international students, the process of learning how others operate is simultaneously a process of reflecting on themselves and forming multifaceted views. This is not a process valuable solely for international students: I believe that a willingness to change and learn is the catalyst needed to unleash creativity and potential in Japan and in other places. For any country, balancing regulation with innovative breakthroughs is a dynamic and difficult task. If Japan can alter its cultural rigidity just enough to allow for greater trial and error, it will find many new opportunities for growth and renewal.

Though a single conversation can hardly be seen as a signal of full-scale change, nonetheless a commitment to open-mindedness, from what I have seen in Japan, seems to be their key to greater progress. To fulfill the promise of a big change, one must focus on smaller steps: Japan's economic success lies with its individual citizens, especially the young entrepreneurs, many of whom are excited and hopeful for a great future within their society. My fascinating encounters with Japanese youth on the Asia Leadership Trek have made me feel cautiously optimistic about Japan's future, as I have seen that they are keeping this hope bright and alive.

Malaysia: An Unequal System

After a bumpy night flight from Jakarta, most of us could barely keep our eyes open when we stumbled off the plane at Kuala Lumpur. Yet when we stepped into the brightly lit interiors of the city's airport, it hardly felt like night-time. Just a couple hours ago, in the Indonesian capital's airport, we had seen travelers dressed like the locals, in moderate, traditional attire. Here in Kuala Lumpur, groups of women fully covered by black burqas pushed trolleys past teenage girls in racerback tanks and thigh-high shorts. Immediately, we could see greater diversity and feel an increase in energy. We knew that this stage of the Trek would be anything but ordinary.

A boost of excitement was injected into our group when we met with the Student Leaders ("SL") from Sunway University. Though it was two o'clock in the morning, their big smiles were as uniform as their crimson t-shirts. All of them were cheering for us after waiting for hours at the arrival area. They took care of our luggage, guided us onto coach buses, and parceled out brown bags with perfectly balanced snacks. We were amazed and delighted by the thoughtfulness that the organizers had put into the program and quickly started to mingle with the SLs. Their warm hospitality was our first impression of Malaysia.

In the following days, our hosts from Sunway University entertained us with an extensive and exquisite line-up of activities, from round-table political talks to waist-high water-cave explorations, from cultural shows performed by diverse ethnic groups to an endless supply of local delicacies. Despite occasional delays, our group managed to stay on top of our packed schedule. Occasionally we felt exhausted, but we could not complain when we heard stories from the SLs of their late nights as they strove to keep the program running smoothly.

We soon found that there was even more depth to their hospitality than we had originally thought. Our hosts were not just guides; they took care of us in every way and felt an obligation to ensure that everything on our trip was flawless. The SLs constantly made compromises to make our experience as close to perfect as possible. The night before our conference, for example, many Trekkers could not find appropriate power adapters. Although this was the sort of problem that savvy travelers should normally take care of themselves, the SAs once again stayed up until the early morning, doing everything they could to get enough adapters for all of us.

It appeared clear to us that, in Malaysia, what is most important is not one's own preferences but the benefit of the group and the fulfillment of duty. In this context, one late arrival, even if caused by a legitimate reason, might seem blameworthy to a Malaysian because of the inconvenience suffered by others. Embracing this relentlessly community-oriented attitude, the Sunway team pulled off another successful Asia Leadership Conference in Kuala Lumpur, with over a thousand participants and hundreds of workshops taught by the Trekkers. The scale and operational complexity was astonishing, and the conference became an achievement that all the organizers took pride in.

Yet, even as we celebrated the success of our efforts, I was shocked to hear from many young and talented students that they wanted to leave Malaysia. When I sat down with some eager participants during the conference and asked them what their ideal futures would be, most of the answers included "going abroad." The seminar participants asked me what careers they should pursue after graduation, but they had little knowledge of their own potential. Instead, they felt stuck in a routine of doing what they "had to do." When I shared personal stories about carving out my own career path in the U.S. and discovering activities that I enjoyed, they gave me looks of disbelief. Despite their excellent English, such ideas were totally foreign to them. What they were certain of was that their own status quo was disappointing and that going abroad would provide them with a meaningful change.

Puzzled by this juxtaposition of diligence and discontent, warmth and distress, I wondered what was keeping these young people—who constitute the driving forces of innovation and progress in a society— from accepting their homeland and believing that it would be the best place to achieve their dreams.

On one of our long bus rides, Laura, a college student studying in KL, described the process of college examinations and admissions in Malaysia. In addition to performing well in an intense, memorization-based system of accumulating GPAs and comprehensive entrance exams, Laura and her sister had to deal with something out of their control: as ethnic minorities, they do not have an equal chance of getting into the public college system, which must reserve a much higher quota for Malaysia's ethnic majority. This revelation piqued my interest. I remembered programs similar to this one in the U.S.

and China, but in both of those cases the quota systems were designed to give ethnic minorities an added advantage. In Malaysia, the quotas' purpose is the opposite. "I wish we felt more peaceful about this problem," Laura said, "but here in Malaysia these types of ethnic issues, especially when it comes to education and employment opportunities, are extremely sensitive. It's very awkward among friends and classmates from different races when we encounter these topics."

Even on a visit of only a few days, we Trekkers could feel this contentiousness. "It's just so unfair" is a common feeling that Laura and many minority students share. The words are simple but powerful. I was aware that ethnic minorities have historically claimed higher incomes in Malaysian society and that there is thus some logic in providing more help to the majority. However, I worry about the restrictions that this policy places on individuals who cannot determine for themselves which group they belong to and are therefore bounded by something they cannot change or control. The sense of fairness and agency that citizens feel directly affects their willingness to work hard and to believe in a positive future for themselves. For Malaysians, the young and bright often find it difficult to find this sense of fairness and hope, and as a result, it is natural that many of them turn to "going abroad" as an appealing alternative.

Malaysian leaders are aware of these challenges and are making strides in changing the status quo. As we learned in our meetings with government ministers, leading officers have turned to best business practices as a means of improving their operations. I heard terms during these meetings that I had previously encountered in the classrooms of the Harvard Business School: culture of meritocracy, clear result measurement, sound incentive design, prudent partnership. Senator Paul Low, Minister of Governance and Integrity, underscored the importance of government integrity during his talk with the ALT team. He mentioned that corruption reaches throughout the political system and that directing transformation from top to bottom would be slow and ineffective. Instead, he argued that instilling a sense of individual responsibility in every minister and clarifying goals at each level would be critical. Similarly, Senator Idris Jala, CEO of Performance Management & Delivery Unit under the Prime Minister's Department, promoted open discussions among cabinet members to determine priorities and introduced colored scorecards for measuring reform results. He argued that to resist inertia, every member of the government system needs to believe that changes today are necessary for a better institution tomorrow.

Despite abundant aspirations among public officials to promote greater accountability and efficiency in the government's operations, the challenge of balancing effective progress with habitual political demands continues to slow the pace of reforms. Intense and pervasive contentiousness—whether it is called "social friction" or "political uncertainty"—ranks among the most frequently cited reasons for diminishing international capital investments and the emigration of talent. Essentially, it is a condition that does not work efficiently or follow market logic, and so return-seeking investors and reward-seeking private citizens cannot expect consistent outcomes for the capital or efforts they put in. These are concepts that I had seen in textbooks, but our visit to Malaysia gave me a vivid glimpse into a real situation that was more convincing than any words or charts.

Here in Malaysia, I first heard the term "democracy without meritocracy"—from a college student. Conversations in KL and Ipoh showed us that ethnic-based biases extend beyond the educational realm into the general labor market. Exclusive access for the ethnic majority to comfortable public-sector jobs or informal government subsidies adds another layer of risk, which hinders growth. The one place where I did see hope of change was in the private sector: Dr. Jeffrey Cheah's business, despite its imperfections, provides an admirable example of meritocracy, upward mobility, and economic success. Specifically, Dr. Cheah told us that to build his business, he hired and promoted people using a color-blind system, without any reference to their ethnicities; he based his hiring decisions solely on capabilities—a stance that many Western countries now often take for granted

Laura was especially struck by the notion of being "color-blind," and after Dr. Cheah's talk she shared with me a probing, self-reflective question: "I wonder if I could really be color-blind." As an ethnic minority with big ambitions, she has been living for a long time with a bitter feeling of unfairness—and there is indeed a great danger, in an unequal society like Malaysia's, that both the habitually mistreated group and the habitually benefited group will lose their ability to think independently, their willingness to change, and their faith in the government's wish to improve the situation. In this sense, they also lose the ability to be truly "color-blind."

What is progress? The Asia Leadership Trek allowed me to progress by experiencing macroeconomic theories in real life, in a region that I care for and connect with. Laura's progress came when she felt challenged by Dr. Cheah's words and realized that things she believed in could be wrong. When a vulnerable individual forms a new willingness to examine truth through different lenses, he or she gains both a deepened understanding and greater opportunities. Such moments of self-examination, felt by vast numbers of people, can lift whole communities onto higher levels of innovation and progress. In Malaysia, we were privileged to witness and experience some of these moments of self-examination and reflection. On a large scale, I believe they will eventually set the country on a better path for becoming a fair and productive society.

Conclusion

In his class entitled "Institutions, Macroeconomics and the Global Economy" at the Harvard Business School, Professor Rafael Di Tella provoked his students with reflections on Argentina's 2001 crisis: "Children were malnourished, and people were dying of hunger from hyper-inflating food price, while the Wall Street financiers bickered and negotiated for debt payment in shiny suit and ties. If this crisis doesn't make your blood boil, I don't know what I can teach you." His rhetoric echoed in my mind as I reflected on my experiences during the Asia Leadership Trek. Before the Trek, my understanding of Asian economic conditions had been limited to numbers and symbols. Once I arrived there, however, concepts I had learned while studying "macro" economics manifested in "micro" experiences: the "conserve energy" signs taped to high-tech hand dryers in Tokyo; the anxious yet hopeful emotions expressed in reunification discussions in Korea; the smiles of excitement from our hosts when I exchanged U.S. dollars bills for their ringgits in Kuala Lumpur; and the bustling flow of motorcycles in the morning traffic in Jakarta.

Having grown up in China but conducted most of my higher education and work experiences in the U.S., I understand the complexity and difficulty of applying prevailing macroeconomic theories to the enormous continent of Asia. In the classic market-oriented framework, price functions smoothly to balance supply and demand, and the invisible hand allocates resources in an orderly manner, ensuring socially favorable outcomes. But in practice these mechanisms meet many limitations in the developing world, where coordination problems and systemic beliefs exert a dramatic influence on economic conditions, and unexpected market failures cause and aggravate situations ranging from mild recessions to full-blown crises.

In my attempt to understand macroeconomics in the developing world during the Asia Leadership Trek, I observed two dominant themes. First, macroeconomics deeply affects the lives of individuals regardless of their level of awareness. I can tangibly measure how much more work I can deliver in heated buildings, where I don't have to run around to keep myself warm and functional, than I could deliver in my earlier years. In textbooks, that phenomenon is represented as an abstraction—the letter A—and dubbed "total factor productivity." Second, it is highly difficult to internalize different world views without diverse and substantial firsthand experiences. For Indonesians who lived through the chaos of 1997, sufficient fuel stands for security. For Chinese who participated in the wave of open-market industrialization, high savings equal prosperity. For our young friends in Malaysia, compromise and racial tolerance are the natural price to pay for peace. Financiers on Wall Street see the gains and losses on their investments as changing numbers on a screen and perhaps as triggers to change jobs or switch houses; such experiences pale in comparison with the pain felt by those lower down on the socio-economic scale, where financial crises translate into hunger, turmoil, and despair.

For many, macroeconomics and policy-making in Asian economies seem too complex, too volatile, and too illogical to understand. But the desire to make progress in Asia is unstoppable. During the Trek I observed that the core motivation of everyone's daily endeavors is simple: they want to do better today than they did yesterday. Understanding this motivation inspired me and made me realize the astonishing intellectual resources that we have today: in examining the economic systems of prosperous countries all around the world—the U.S., Germany, Japan—we can analyze them, test them, and change them as we imagine new economic paths for each country in Asia. Our motivation in doing so is simple and universally human: we all want to learn from the best.

When I returned from the Trek, I felt a strong desire to keep sharing, rethinking, and reflecting on what I learned in Asia. The constant testing of my prior knowledge in macroeconomics has made me lean towards the notion that no one theory or system of beliefs can be universally correct in our complex world. When applying different tools and formulating economic policies, the most efficient method may not be the most executable, and the most executable may not be the most just. Perhaps the best step toward progress is the somber but liberating acknowledgment that we can always be wrong. As when Taka learned about Japan's history from a different country, or when Laura asked herself if she had the ability to be racially blind, painful yet revelatory moments often act as keys to unlock new ideas and new solutions. To me, these moments offer a path to greater enlightenment, to the possibility of understanding phenomena beyond one's own experiences, and to greater prosperity in any market and society.

As countries in Asia become more connected with each other and the rest of the world—either in person, virtually, or by association—their populations' worldviews and methods of economic development will also expand. And I am confident that as each Asian country's cultural perspectives diversify and strengthen, so will its capacity for learning, innovation, and growth.

Chapter 2

Understanding Indonesian Entrepreneurship through Foreign Eyes and Paradigms

Alanna Hughes

MPA, Harvard Kennedy School of Government

MBA, MIT Sloan School of Management

● ● ●

I could take the heat: that dense, tropical, island humidity that breathes down your neck from dawn until dusk. I could take the chaos: horns blaring as taxis bottleneck in busy intersections, street vendors overtaking any hint of sidewalk to pitch dining tents and refreshment kiosks, auto-rickshaws and motorcycles weaving through (and in front of) trucks and buses free of trepidation or apology. From the first day, it was easy to feel that I "got" Indonesia: another middle-income island economy, another rapidly urbanizing capital city endeavoring to accommodate migration, growth, and globalization in today's fast-paced world. My first twenty-four hours in-country made me long for the country I often use as my direct comparison: my second home, the Dominican Republic, where I worked and lived for the majority of my pre-graduate-school career.

It took Skye Bar's blast of crisp, late-night air to wake me from my presumptions. Our first two days in Jakarta had been jam-packed: from visits to major government agencies and corporations to running a conference at a university outside the city, we had spent hours navigating traffic and crossing our fingers that we would get to our appointments on time. Tonight, I finally had the opportunity to sneak away with a few of my MIT Sloan classmates and grab a drink with some alumni of our MBA program who were working in the capital.

Ears popping, I arrived on the fifty-sixth floor and stepped into one of the swankiest places in Jakarta for urban professionals and international guests. Moving through the interior—the expensively stocked bar with its mixologists concocting special libations, the dimly lit lounge dotted with patrons in sleek corporate or party-going attire—I stepped out onto the patio to take in the skyline. A chill went down my spine as I ventured into the open air; this high up, this late at night, the heat to which I was accustomed was nowhere to be found. Nor were the "fixtures" I had already begun to take for granted in the streets: the sellers, the buyers, the drivers, the passengers. Instead, what I saw was a series of networks: interlinked streets and highways, colored by the lights of towers, restaurants, apartment buildings, and hotels in addition to headlights, stoplights, and neon signs. From up here I could see almost the entire city—and what a stunning view it was!

I needed this breath of fresh air and this bird's-eye view to remind me of why I had come on the Asia Leadership Trek in the first place. For years before entering graduate school, I had worked both as a social entrepreneur and as an advisor to smaller-scale entrepreneurs. In my interview for business school, my interviewer had suggested that graduate studies could be a time for me to "upward periscope"—to take a step back and see the bigger picture, the systems level of new business creation and growth. Since arriving at MIT and HKS, I have taken this advice seriously, discovering frameworks for thinking about how different players within a society need to work together to foster new opportunities and economic growth. In my trip through Asia—since I had neither a deep knowledge of the region nor the time to learn in detail about its economies—I hoped instead to take a larger view and observe how different societal actors—individuals, companies, the government, academic institutions, and financiers—interconnect to form complex economic systems. I hoped to offer a fresh perspective on how they might tighten their collaborations to further encourage entrepreneurial activity. As a professional, I had been used to being the one on the ground, with all the details in hand. In this experience, however, I was able to use cultural and experiential distance and difference to connect the dots, just as the lights along the skyline on that beautiful, clear Jakarta night formed an interconnected pattern when I saw them from above.

● ● ●

Beauty is in the eye of the beholder, and in order to understand my reflections on the vibrancy of Indonesia's budding entrepreneurial ecosystem it is important to know the personal experiences that frame my thinking. Prior to graduate school, I worked for five years in international development and social entrepreneurship in Washington, D.C. and parts of the Latin American and Caribbean regions. As a young professional, I was fortunate to have the opportunity to see both the forests and the trees. During my time at the global headquarters of Ashoka: Innovators for the Public, arguably the first organization to identify and invest in leading social entrepreneurs, I gained exposure to support for entrepreneurship at the systems level; this type of thinking took the new idea out of a vacuum and challenged it against other influencers of success: How did the social entrepreneurship model compare to others? What partners—nonprofit, for profit, or government—would help the innovator bring the idea to scale? How would the innovator financially back his or her idea? What made the idea innovative in the first place, and what characteristics of the social entrepreneur and the environment in which he or she worked facilitated the ability to adapt and stay on the forefront?

I have also had the privilege of walking in both entrepreneurs' and social entrepreneurs' shoes, predominantly in other island economies. As a newly minted college graduate, I began my career as a Community Economic Development Volunteer in the Peace Corps, spending two years coaching established and aspiring entrepreneurs in launching and managing businesses in the Dominican Republic. After Ashoka, I returned to the island of Hispaniola to launch the first branch of a social enterprise, Community Enterprise Solutions, in both the D.R. and Haiti. Although these experiences put me elbow-deep into the day-to-day challenges that an entrepreneur faces, I did not lose sight of the bigger picture. The ability of new models to succeed depends not only on the minds and ambitions of the people who introduce them but also on other societal players across the fields of education, government, business, and finance. For example, my primary project in the Peace Corps, a community-based agrotourism project called the "Chocolate Tour"—which showed where chocolate comes from, how it is commercialized, and how its sales improve well-being in sourcing communities—succeeded not solely because the idea itself was innovative for that part of the world; it also relied upon key investors, received various forms of endorsement from the Dominican and American governments, and gained access to partnerships with existing companies such as tour operators.

My perspective, shaped by the aforementioned opportunities and experiences, found validation the semester before I set out on the Asia Leadership Trek via an MIT course called the "Regional Entrepreneurship Acceleration Lab" (or "REAL" for short). REAL asked a question relevant to Indonesia's case, the Dominican Republic's case, my home country's case, and those of countless other parts of the world: how can we accelerate innovation-driven entrepreneurship to create vibrant regional economies? Amazingly enough, REAL answered the question through a framework similar to the one I had begun to develop intuitively during the course of my professional experiences: a five-player "Innovation Ecosystem Stakeholder Model." In order for a country to develop innovations successfully from inception to the market (an ability that REAL calls "I-Cap") and for it to start and build new businesses from inception to maturity (an ability that REAL calls "E-Cap"), it must possess not only capable, motivated entrepreneurs but also government, corporate, university, and risk-capital support.

It was with this five-angled viewpoint that I entered Indonesia, ready to learn more about how each of these actors functioned, independently and together, to support the creation and growth of new businesses that can influence not only Indonesia but the ASEAN region and the rest of the world. What follows is a discussion of what I observed, from both the street and my elevated vantage point, and of the entrepreneurial potential that Indonesia currently holds.

Figure 1 Framework used by MIT's Regional Entrepreneurship Acceleration Program (REAP)[1]

Entrepreneurs

To analyze Indonesia's entrepreneurial scene solely by reflecting upon my interactions with the entrepreneurs I met would be like trying to understand Jakarta solely through the *kakilimas* lining the

---

1   This framework is used by MIT's Regional Entrepreneurship Acceleration Program (REAP). Additional information can be found on REAP's homepage at http://reap.mit.edu/about/.

congested streets; both play invaluable roles within their own ecosystems, but they could not function in isolation. However, like local business owners, the entrepreneurs developing Innovation-Driven Enterprises (IDEs) in Indonesia can illustrate a lot about their country's values and trajectory. I was able to get a glimpse of Indonesia's diversity through the diversity of ideas among the entrepreneurs we spoke with.

I had heard ahead of time that most Indonesian entrepreneurs are currently focusing on technology companies, perhaps with the aspiration to create an ASEAN Silicon Valley. Our visit to Tiket.com, an Indonesian online travel-reservation system much like Expedia, Kayak, and Hipmunk in the U.S., reinforced this impression. From the moment we walked into its office in downtown Jakarta, I felt as though I had been teleported to Palo Alto. Walking through the rooms of the multi-level, airy office, located in a relatively residential part of the city, I went through a mental checklist of similarities with the start-ups I had visited on MIT Sloan's Silicon Valley tour. A catchy, colorful logo on the wall and on employee t-shirts? Check. Open spaces for collaboration? Check. Free meals to keep employees motivated and focused? Check. Rows of computers for big-data analytics, programming, customer-service tasks, and other facets of the business? Check, check, check. Even the presentation we received felt in line with an investor pitch one might hear in California: Jakarta has the tenth largest airport in the world, with an expected 20 percent growth; Indonesia's domestic market of 72.5 million passengers is the fifth largest in the world; Tiket.com is capitalizing on this demand by providing tickets for regional and international airlines, serving as the top online agent for Indonesia's major train company, and localizing its services for everything from accepting mobile money payments to leveraging its platform to sell tickets for shows and concerts.

Yet, just as I was tempted to write off Tiket.com and Indonesia's start-up scene as another example of the "copy-cat venture" trend, our hosts shed light on realities unique to their country. Halting the PowerPoint presentation to call upon eager Trek visitors, the team spoke with candor about the outflow of capital since the 1998 financial crisis, the limited capacity of Indonesia's servers (which is such that Tiket.com depends on servers in Singapore), and the fact that 70 percent of Indonesia's GDP is consumption—not a bad thing within the scope of a domestically focused company, but definitely something to bear in mind when determining what product or service to bring to market and whether to focus on domestic or foreign customers.

I left that meeting both intrigued by the commonalities that superseded geographic location and determined to think more deeply about the degree to which Indonesia's entrepreneurial diversity matched the archipelago's ethnic diversity. Luckily, we had two other meetings that further stretched my thinking as well as my international network.

From the minute I stepped into the reception hosted by HIPMI, I felt at ease. Having spent several years working with entrepreneurs outside of the U.S., I was accustomed to making small talk with members of associations seated at small tables and snacking on whatever refreshments were provided. Although surprised that the treat of choice looked like a fast-food falafel, I was happy to grab a juice and make myself at home in an empty seat at one of the round tables.

I did not get far into conversation with the entrepreneurs at my table—who, coincidentally, were also the owners of tech companies—

when we were asked to quiet down for a sort of keynote speech: one of the association's most successful entrepreneurs was going to share his business model, his successes, and where he stood in the global scaling process. When he pulled up his logo—red and yellow, with something that looked like a smoking burrito—it dawned on me that the man behind the podium was also behind the Middle-Eastern nibbles on our table. Mr. Hendy Setiono, founder of Kebab Turki Baba Rafi, is responsible for what is now the world's largest kebab chain. Beginning as a single food cart in 2003, his company is now a franchisee model providing more than one thousand two hundred kebab outlets in Indonesia and seven other countries. Clearly, Indonesia's entrepreneurial ecosystem offered a pathway to success that innovation-driven businesses, even those not grounded in technology, could follow. Setiono's ambition to create the world's largest kebab chain identified an opportunity unmet by the McDonalds, Burger Kings, and KFCs of the world, and it also defied my initial impressions of Indonesia's entrepreneurial climate as a Silicon-Valley imitation. I hoped that my assumptions would be further tested. I also regretted choosing a beverage over food when I walked in—Setiono was obviously doing something right, because his sandwiches were all gone by the time he finally whetted my appetite.

If I did not expect to find inspiration in fast food, I certainly did not expect it in beauty products; but our visit to Mustika Ratu painted a third, very different picture of what Indonesian entrepreneurship can look like. Toward the end of yet another meeting-filled day, I was looking forward to visiting the spa for a massage. Stepping into the lobby of Taman Sari Royal Heritage Spa and absorbing my surroundings—the sight of tasteful wooden fixtures, the smell of fresh cut flowers and aromatic oils, the taste of freshly brewed herbal tea, and the sound of local musicians chiming on traditional percussion instruments—I felt serenity wash away my stress.

I expected to relax my muscles, but in Mustika Ratu I instead stimulated my brain. Through the eyes of Ms. Putir K. Wardani, the CEO of the spa, I and my fellow Trekkers gained a sense of what it's like not only to scale a beauty-products business to an international level, but also to be a female entrepreneur in Indonesia. Although the country is in some ways one of the most tolerant in the world, disparities still persist. The International Labor Organization notes that gender discrimination is one of the primary drivers behind Indonesia's sex-segregated labor market and that men and women have to face numerous gender issues differently.[2] Given that the majority of Indonesian entrepreneurs are still male, what is creating the bottleneck and how can women overcome it? Ms. Wardani's team comprises a group of smart, motivated former Miss Indonesia contestants, a team that highlights by contrast cultural norms—such as the fact that many women are still reluctant to show strength and confidence, and that traditionally women have been expected to take care of the house and children—and resultant behaviors: approximately 30 percent of Indonesian women stop working when they get married, and another estimated 30 percent stop working after they have children. All of these factor make it more difficult for women to launch IDEs. Wardani's spa has created new luxury products and services and offers a new model for international joint ventures, but she succeeded only

---

2   This and additional information can be found on ILO's "Equality and Discrimination" page at http://ilo.org/jakarta/areasofwork/equality-and-discrimination/lang--en/index.html.

by overcoming hurdles that a man with tantamount ambition would not have encountered.

While our interactions with these three diverse entrepreneurial ventures—Tiket.com, Kebab Turki Baba Rafi, and Mustika Ratu—came nowhere close to covering the whole gamut of entrepreneurship in Indonesia, they went a long way toward convincing me of three major points: first, Indonesian individuals with ideas for new businesses are now in a society in which they can make their ideas reality; second, though technology might be a primary innovation driver, many Indonesian entrepreneurs are building scalable businesses focused on other industries and other forms of competitive advantage; and third, although—as in the U.S. and other nations throughout the world—there is still much to be done in Indonesia to empower female entrepreneurs, it is nonetheless possible for them to flourish within the country's current entrepreneurial ecosystem.

What are some of the larger factors that have made these developments possible? It is important to understand how other players contribute to entrepreneurial dynamism, for there is more to each of these stories than simply an individual effecting change.

Risk Capital

Tiket.com, Kebab Turki Baba Rafi, and Mustika Ratu are success stories for many reasons, perhaps first and foremost because they have become profitable operations. I was anxious to learn more about the dynamics of financing entrepreneurial ventures within Indonesia's fast-growing economy.

One morning, I arose earlier than the other Trekkers to set off on a mini adventure. Descending to the modern-chic lobby of the Mercure in which we were staying, I approached the receptionist with my biggest smile. "Hello," I began. "I need a taxi to take me to Pacific Place; I do not speak Bahasa, but I hope that you can help me navigate my way to the Coffee Bean."

After a nod and a quick phone call, the receptionist shuttled me into a metered vehicle and waved me off. Once again, I found myself weaving through unfamiliar congested streets—only this time I was completely alone. Bereft of my fellow Trekkers or local MIT Sloan contacts, I could only hope that my driver knew the direction we needed to take to reach our destination.

Fortunately, finding the posh, towering Pacific Place did not pose much of a challenge; harder to locate was the right entrance for my meeting point. After English and hand gestures failed me, I eventually got out of the cab and looped around the complex myself, being careful not to sweat too much in my suit nor catch the pavement the wrong way in my heels.

As I stepped through the door of the Coffee Bean, blotting my face with a napkin to remove perspiration and exhaust, I recognized the irony of my morning's journey thus far. In a sense, it felt analogous to what I was here to investigate: when an individual or team begins an entrepreneurial journey with a new idea, the person or group often needs support to set the venture off on the right track. Would I encounter this risk-capital support within Indonesia's entrepreneurial ecosystem? I threw away my napkin, donned my smile once more, and sat down with a Managing Partner from Ideosource to find out.

Although Ideosource is only one player within a spectrum of potential financiers in Indonesia, meeting with one of its partners was a fabulous way to learn about the current state of risk capital for start-ups in the country's dynamic emerging market. Over an iced coffee that cost more than my twenty-minute cab ride, Edward told me first about Ideosource's short history. The firm was founded through money raised among family and friends in 2011 and began as a consulting company, though it transitioned into being a venture-capital firm after a friend working in a private-equity firm predicted that venture capital would be the next big thing for Indonesia's economy: internet penetration was expected to double over the next four to five years, and Indonesia's GDP per capita had passed $3,000 USD (which some analysts claim is a magic number for rising into the middle class). By pushing to the frontier of change, Ideosource found a place at the center of Tech in Asia's first "start-up Asia" event in 2012, when very few foreign investors were interested in Indonesian early-stage companies.

But Ideosource's time in the limelight did not last long. Since 2012, many more investors and incubators have entered Indonesia, including, among others, the Founder Institute, Start-Up Bootcamp, and several Japanese, European, and American investors. Ideosource has since stopped incubating new businesses and has honed in instead on its venture investments, offering investments of $150,000 instead of $50,000 to provide a longer runway (of approximately eighteen months) that reduces chances of early failure.

As the moment approached when I would need to reunite with the other Trekkers, I mulled over Edward's insights. First, a lot of Indonesian VC funds closed down in 2013—was this because portfolio companies still had limited exposure to what start-ups need to become self-sustaining? was it because the relatively new entrepreneurial ecosystem struggled to provide companies with follow-on investments? or had it happened for some other reason? Secondly, no Indonesian company has gone public in the current economic landscape; several have been acquired, but entrepreneurs and investors should be aiming for IPOs within the next couple years.

Jittery from caffeine and from the rush of an informative, independent adventure, I shook Edward's hand and walked away, pondering my new knowledge. While congestion and speed bumps still hinder Indonesian entrepreneurs from receiving the financing that will allow them to move at full speed, nonetheless the road to risk capital seems to be smoothing out, as companies gain traction and both domestic and international financers learn from mistakes and best practices.

Government

The tall, white, Romanesque columns, perched above a perfectly manicured lawn, offered a dramatic contrast to Pacific Palace's ubermodern façade. Nonetheless, when I stepped into the majestic home of the Indonesian Ministry of Foreign Affairs, I knew that I would soon acquire another lens through which to view Indonesian entrepreneurship.

Before the Head of Policy Analysis entered the meeting room, I took the opportunity to survey my surroundings: a big, U-shaped conference table adorned with microphones; portraits of notable politicians; courtesy snack boxes as place markers for every visitor. Acutely aware of how "governmental" the room felt, I compared it with the casual, open, and minimalist layouts of the start-up offices I had visited less than a year ago on MIT Sloan's Silicon Valley tour.

The Ministry's more formal décor reminded me that I was, after all, on a policy school visit.

Our host, however, quickly demonstrated the connections between policy and entrepreneurship. Presenting President Jokowi's foreign policy of "trisakti"—"three powers"—Dr. Darmansjah Djumala emphasized that one of these three pillars is self-reliance within Indonesia's economy. Because Indonesia is a rising middle power, it must pursue "prosperity" (economic development) hand-in-hand with "sovereignty" (legal and political considerations). One of the administration's focuses is to empower the "*wong cilik*" or the "little" (poor) people, a category that includes small and medium enterprises (SMEs). While these microentrepreneurs are important, however, what about those with more ambitious plans for ventures on a regional, national, and/or global scale? Dr. Djumala acknowledged that Indonesia has traditionally produced for the domestic market instead of exporting; its middle class, comprising 52 percent of Indonesia's population, has a high purchasing power. Nevertheless, the government is actively supporting the development of a high-tech industry in cooperation with South Korea and Japan, among other countries.

During our next meeting, with Dr. Dino Patti Djalal, we learned a sobering fact: only approximately four hundred thousand of Indonesia's two hundred fifty million people are currently IDE entrepreneurs. Indonesia aims to raise this number to 1-2 percent of its population, but it has a long way to go. Given that another 57 million people in the country run SMEs, part of the goal should be to help these individuals scale up—for example, through microcredit. Another intervention, with increasing power, stems from Indonesian universities, which are moving into teaching technological entrepreneurship.

By the time we exited the building, I felt confident that the Indonesian government was attempting to bolster small businesses, as with their creation of fishing villages for existing and potential fishermen and women. Still, they could certainly do more to help new ideas grow into big, transformative ventures. Ultimately, the advice I would most like to give Indonesia's government is a statement made by one my former employers: "Our job is not to give people fish, and it's not to teach them how to fish; it's to build new and better fishing industries"—in this case, ones that are more innovative, more profitable, and more impactful at a larger scale.[3]

Corporate and University

In our four, jam-packed days in Jakarta, we Trekkers managed to visit two large corporations that shape media and energy in Indonesia and one university just outside the capital. While our conversations at these places did not focus directly on innovation-driven entrepreneurship, our discussions, encounters with current leaders and students, and immersion in their offices and campuses enabled me to find many sources of connection with Indonesia's entrepreneurs.

SCTV and MedcoEnergi are two vastly different Indonesian enterprises. SCTV—Surya Citra Televisi—has become a major Indonesian TV channel since its founding in 1990. Its parent company, Emtek, is the second largest media group in Indonesia; it runs this channel, provides media consulting and media communications services to

---

3   https://ashoka.org/entrepreneurforsociety.

other companies, and manages "Solutions" and "Connectivity" business divisions that covering everything from infrastructure to retail services.[4] MedcoEnergi, on the other hand, is a publicly listed Indonesian oil and gas company founded in 1980. Given the two companies' differences, I was surprised to find commonalities in terms of what they could offer to the growing entrepreneurial ecosystem. Stepping into each posh, modern high-rise in Central Jakarta, I realized that these companies each provided an example of the scale to which new entrepreneurs should aspire. In the decades that they have been in existence, the two have succeeded in becoming highly profitable leaders in their respective industries, on a national and international scale. Whether sitting in the brightly lit recording studios at SCTV or chatting over dinner with MedcoEnergi's executives, who had flown in from all over the archipelago, I sensed the depth of resources and expertise that each of these companies can provide to those who are just starting out.

To date, these companies have engaged with entrepreneurs of varying scales; for example, MedcoEnergi provides microfinancing to small-scale companies as part of its sustainable growth strategy, and SCTV made a series-B investment in a local online marketplace, BukaLapak, just last month. Each of these two companies possesses the potential to be a powerful investor in new ideas. Additionally, both of them could take another step to mentor and incubate new ventures that crop up in their own industries. Although this may sound like breeding competition, it might in fact have the opposite effect: MedcoEnergi and SCTV could help entrepreneurs grow businesses that

---

4   http://www.emtek.co.id/About-Us-(1)/About-the-Company.aspx.

relate to their core competencies, with the hope of eventually acquiring them, forming a joint venture, or contracting their services. This is just the tip of the iceberg for Indonesia's lucrative corporations, which have the privilege of viewing society from the top.

● ● ●

When I stepped onto the grounds of Universitas Pelita Harapan (UPH)—although the campus was clean, green, and located well outside the chaos of the city center—I could still sense the familiar bustle of ambition and excitement emanating from the students who rushed among the class-buildings, athletic facilities, and student center.

Through our half-day conference for young adults, I hoped to pinpoint the degree of entrepreneurial spirit existing in the student body. As it turned out, in such a short amount of time the level of enthusiasm was tough to gauge; nevertheless, I attempted to read between the lines whenever possible. During our keynotes and panels, UPH's students impressed me with their challenging questions—they were certainly thinking creatively about the problems they observed. When we divided into smaller groups for a series of workshops, I chose to shadow a friend running a session on social entrepreneurship. Seated in a stiff desk at the back of a classroom, I listened as the students came up with their own ideas for social ventures. Chatter buzzed as the participants collaborated in small teams to come up with concepts that met needs they cared about. Yet, when it came time to present their solutions in front of the room, most sat silently, their hands glued to their sides and their eyes focused anywhere but on the facilitator.

This seemingly counterintuitive combination of eagerness and reluctance encouraged me to conduct more research on Indonesia's entrepreneurship pedagogy. Although I cannot claim to be an expert on UPH, I noticed when reading through their course descriptions online that they embrace "entrepreneurial spirit" as part of the curriculum. From the descriptions, however, it appears that most of this "spirit" is focused on family businesses as opposed to larger-scale IDEs.[5] Based on my reading on Indonesian learning approaches, I surmise that campuses need to encourage more "outside the box" thinking; Indonesia has received criticism for "teaching to the test" and favoring rote learning and memorization over problem-solving. One potential model for overcoming this restrictive system was created by a successful entrepreneur named Ciputra, a sort of Indonesian Donald Trump who has launched a university for entrepreneurship in Surabaya called "Universitas Ciputra." Convinced that Indonesian universities tend to train students to be employees rather than entrepreneurs, Ciputra aspires to assist pupils in starting high-growth, innovative companies.[6] His approach is one that I believe could be woven into the curriculum of most academic institutions; At MIT, for example, we foster innovation, R&D, and venture creation through a holistic set of offerings: not just classes but business-plan competitions, seed funding, accelerators, venture-mentoring advisors and services, technical-skill building, and assistance in team formation. These opportunities—and a population of solutions-oriented students that tend to take risks and think creatively—generate a culture of hacking,

---

5   http://medan.uph.edu/component/wmcontents/content/7/12.html.
6   http://techcrunch.com/2010/06/06/can-indonesias-ciputra-prove-that-great-entrepreneurs-are-made-not-born/.

iteration, and trial and error until success is reached.

Indonesia is starting to develop each piece of this educational puzzle in isolation. For example, Binus University and Multimedia Nusantara University have both launched technology venture accelerators, and some conferences have already been held to enable stakeholders to collaborate on entrepreneurial curricula development. But there remain ample opportunities to put all of the pieces together, giving students a more complete picture of what it takes to form, launch, and scale an IDE.[7] Recalling the intent expressions of the students listening while we presented during our conference, I am confident that there is a lot of interest among Indonesian youth in learning new ways to change the world and to obtain financial and reputational prosperity. But, as I learned first in my REAL course at MIT, putting these ambitions into practice requires the collaboration of governments, VCs, corporations, and universities, so that academic-level entrepreneurial ecosystems can feed into the country's broader economic landscape.

Conclusion

The fascinating thing about being fifty-six stories up is that you feel you can see everything: from our lookout, I swear I could pinpoint the commercial façade of Pacific Place, the stately architecture of the government compounds, and even the lights of our trendy hotel. Yet, although I could connect the dots with roadways, streetlights,

---

7   https://www.techinasia.com/binus-accelerator-tech-startup/; http://www.gew.co/blog/stakeholders-indonesia-collaborate-entrepreneurial-nation.

billboards, and even the headlights of motorcycles and taxis below, everything still felt a little hazy. In a way our four days in Jakarta were like that: there was so much to see and take in at the ground level that I do not yet feel I have the expertise to give an authoritative judgment on Indonesia's entrepreneurial ecosystem, as I would for, say, the Dominican Republic. Nevertheless, because of my unique perspective—shaped by my experiences in other parts of the world, my educational background, and the passions I possess—I hope that my observations of how Indonesia's economic and entrepreneurial pieces fit together, and how they can continue to grow and reinforce each other, hold some value. I will not forget the ideas I heard for making the country's entrepreneurial ecosystem more robust. For example, Edward, the partner at Ideosource, speculated that the government could provide greater intellectual-property certainty, bring in more people from industry to shape the policies that affect new business creation, and offer financial incentives for new companies with promising business models (as Israel and Singapore have done). It is inspiring to know th ese ideas sprang from only one among hundreds of eager innovators within Indonesia.

Perhaps my role, as an outsider, is not so much to aid in creating the system as to foster such connections within it: I am pleased to have urged Edward to think about what advice he would give to the government regarding entrepreneurship. I hope that my analysis and my journey will help others think about future collaboration opportunities between sectors, in order to found and support Indonesian IDEs that can influence global markets. Up on the fifty-sixth floor in the Skye Bar, I felt certain that when I left Indonesia, I would depart with a sense of optimism about its entrepreneurial potential. And that thought—along with the cool night breeze and the swanky cocktail in my hand—was utterly refreshing.

| Chapter 3 |

The Modern Philippines:
How a Nation Raised by the Spanish Empire and the U.S. Grew Into Its Own

Greg Manne

Ed.M., Harvard Graduate School of Education

● ● ●

Introduction

"The Philippines—it's like Hollywood meets the Spanish Inquisition," said a former U.S. Ambassador in a private, pre-departure meeting with members of the 2015 Asia Leadership Trek. As an American with a passion for Spain and its culture, I knew from the moment I joined the Trek that the Philippines was going to be one of the countries that most intrigued me on our tour.

After a long day of wandering in and out of old churches and forts in *intramuros*, the historic center of Manila, I sat with a group of my fellow Trekkers at a restaurant, enjoying a San Miguel *serbesa* (the local word for beer) and waiting for our server. I was trying to decide which of the pork options on the menu—including chicharon, adobo, and lechon—I might like best, and I also noticed the special on the dessert list: flan. As the waiter approached I reminded myself that I must order in English, not Spanish, because I was in the Philippines, even though numerous encounters during the day had made me feel that I had just spent the afternoon touring a Spanish city.

The next morning we arrived at the SM Mall of Asia, late because of traffic that was hauntingly similar to that of Los Angeles during rush hour. The SM Mall, one of sixteen Metro super malls in Manila, is routinely packed with people waiting in line for breakfast at McDonald's or Burger King, drinking coffee at Starbucks, and visiting shops like Bose and Adidas. The complex boasts all the traditional mall features, including air-conditioning and Wi-Fi as well as leisure pursuits—a movie theater, a bowling alley, and an ice-skating rink. The place was packed with young people and plastered with advertisements featuring thin, light-skinned models (Marshall, 2014). This time I had to remind myself that I was in Manila, not Southern California.

As an undergraduate I studied at an American university and, like many other Americans, spent a semester studying abroad in Spain. Upon graduating from college, I earned a Fulbright Scholarship to teach and conduct research in Madrid. Thus I spent the two years prior to attending the Harvard Graduate School of Education learning the language, culture, and history of a former empire that had a greater impact on the settling of the Americas than perhaps any other nation. Although my formative experiences in Spain took place during and after college, my connection to the nation, its language, culture, and food can be traced back to my childhood. I was born and raised in South Florida, a region that ranks third in Spanish-speaking populations in the United States, located in a state named by Spanish conquistadors containing many historic and cultural remnants of the Spanish empire (U.S. Census Bureau, 2010).

As a graduate student and certified secondary school history teacher, much of my past academic and cultural research has focused on Spanish and American history. Although these two nations are dramatically different in numerous ways, there are several moments in history when their cultural influences converged—and no other place on earth is more representative of this cultural intertwining than the Philippines. Examining the effects of the relationships between the Philippines and its colonial "parents" allows one to understand how the relatively young nation was able to shed its long-held title of "the sick man of Asia" and, in the last five years, to emerge miraculously as the economic "strong man" of Southeast Asia.

Three Hundred Years in a Spanish Convent

What's in a name? I pondered this question as I walked along with my fellow Trekkers, listening to a historical reenactment by Mr. Carlos Celdran—a famous Filipino "tour guide, cultural activist, and performing artist"—and growing ever more aware of the linguistic and cultural connections between Spain and the Philippines. Before I arrived in Manila, our first stop on the Trek, I already knew that the original name, *Islas Filipinas,* had been given to the country by sixteenth-century Spanish conquistadors in homage to King Phillip II of Spain. However, Mr. Celdran offered me and my colleagues an entirely different perspective on this history during his "If These Walls Could Talk" performance in the old, historic center of Manila. The area, known as *intramuros,* translates from the Spanish to "between walls."

If the walls in Manila could talk, their first language would be Spanish, for the walls did not exist prior to the arrival of the conquistadors. Over the centuries, innumerable "Western" terms and ideas from the Spanish language have infiltrated the local language of the Philippines, Tagalog. Mr. Celdran explained that while many of the words in Tagalog for organic things like happiness and love are rooted in the eastern Austronesian languages, dating back thousands of years, such Tagalog words as street (*kalye*), constitution (*konstitusyon*), republic (*republika),* and monarchy (*monarkiya*) are directly rooted in the Spanish language. Through my own research I found another important Tagalog word originating in Spanish: *Ekonomiya* is the Tagalog spelling of *economía,* the Spanish word for economy.

At every stage of our Trek we learned about the complex issues that arise from the concentration of financial power and resources into the hands of a few. This concentration is often faced by former Spanish colonies around the globe. Thus, in order to understand the modern Filipino economy, one must look back to the influence of the Spanish colonists, who brought their economic principles to the islands. Severe inequality is the most pressing economic issue in the Philippines today, and this inequality stems from the societal hierarchy introduced by the Spanish. For hundreds of years, the wealthiest and most powerful people in the country were direct descendants of the Spanish nobility; they had exclusive access to royal capital and were exempt from paying taxes to the crown. The Spanish system of colonization, as seen in much of Latin America, often involved a feudal system that chartered land to those with connections to the Spanish throne and the Church leadership (Francisco and Arriola, 1987). This system laid a foundation for future inequality because it stratified society into two groups: a small, landed oligarchy and the poor, peasant masses. According to U.S. Ambassador Mr. Philip S. Golberg, whom we met with on the first day of the Trek, today just thirty companies control thirty-five percent of the Filipino economy (Goldberg, 2015). The rampant inequality has also perpetuated widespread corruption, a major problem that emanates from the concentration of economic power in the hands of the elite.

Although Spanish colonialism clearly contributed to the present-day economic inequality in the Philippines, it also opened the door for a modern economic success stories. During the Trek my colleagues and I met with Mr. Jamie Auguosto Ayala, CEO of the oldest Filipino company. The Ayala Group was an original benefactor of the colonial agricultural system and has been in existence for nearly two hundred years. In this time the Ayala Group has modernized and diversified, becoming a conglomerate that is now a national leader in the banking, property, construction, telecommunications, electronics, and utilities industries. According to *The Economist*, the current CEO, Mr. Ayala—a graduate of the Harvard Business School—has moved his nation in a new direction by looking for "fortune at the bottom of the economic pyramid" and attempting to open up the economy to those with the fewest resources.

In recent years, the Ayala Group has entered into a number of Public Private Partnerships (PPPs) with local and national governments, bringing clean, running water to more than eight million consumers who previously had none and building housing, schools, and churches in the growing manufacturing and call-center regions outside of Manila. The Ayala Group endeavors to deliver more than just modern products and benefits to its customers. It also recruits local talent into the company's workforce, pays for domestic and international professional education for employees, and offers opportunities for members of the Filipino diaspora to return to the country for higher-paid managerial positions, opportunities that in previous decades did not exist. The Ayala Group, with its legacy as a member of the exclusionary establishment during the Spanish colonial era, is now working to increase economic access for Filipinos in the middle and working classes.

As important as the Spanish colonists' legacy of feudal hierarchy is the legacy of their Roman Catholic religion. The Philippines has a population of ninety-nine million people, 86 percent of whom are Catholic. Some argue that historically *Las Islas Filipinas* were more of a "Catholic" colony than a Spanish one: the islands were left under the sole control of church officials after it was found that they lacked the bullion the Spanish Monarchy craved and tirelessly extracted from its colonies in Central and South America. "All souls but no gold," Carlos told us, describing the situation of the Philippines as an Iberian-Catholic colony with many possible converts but few valuable resources. The concept of the Philippines as a "colony of the Catholic Church" begs the question: How did three centuries in a "convent" affect the modern Filipino economy?

One undeniable impact of pervasive Catholicism in the Philippines has been exponential population growth. In the mid-1970s both the Philippines and Thailand had populations of approximately forty-five million people. Later in our Trek, we learned that, under the direction of HKS graduate and social activist Mr. Mechai Viravaidya (known to many as "Mr. Condom"), the Buddhist nation of

Thailand introduced a persistent and successful population-control program. During his presentation to the ALT Trekkers in Bangkok, Mr. Viravaidya juxtaposed the case of growth in Thailand with that of the Philippines: "Today Thailand has a population of 67 million, while the population of the more religiously conservative Philippines has ballooned to slightly below one hundred million." In the Philippines, we met several Filipino politicians and political ministers who identified the lack of population control as one of numerous failures of the Marcos regime, which held power in the Philippines during the time when Mr. Viravaidya was instituting his program in Thailand. Marcos, as well as some of the democratically elected governments that followed the dictator's regime, made attempts to institute population-control measures, but these failed in the face of considerable pressure from the Catholic Church (*PBS Newshour*, 2014).

Population growth has been a driving force behind several trends in the Filipino economy. Economic inequality, a lack of basic resources (classrooms, textbooks, medicine), and a dearth of domestic-employment opportunities are all lasting effects of a burgeoning population. This growth has also contributed to a "brain drain," as many educated Filipinos immigrate to other nations in search of employment. Not all of the effects are negative, however. Although brain drains are often viewed as a disadvantage, the Filipino diaspora, created by the ten million people who have left to find employment abroad, has aided the growth of the domestic economy via remittances, which make up about ten percent of annual GDP. Moreover, the exponential growth of the population has resulted in a large consumer market, comprising predominantly young people (their average age is twenty-three) who have significant spending power, something that international businesses are eager to access (Macaranas, 2015).

One lasting effect of Iberian-Catholic colonial era in the Philippines that can be considered purely positive is the culture of strong family values and solidarity. In the Philippines, as in Spain, it is common for three generations of family members to live in the same household. During hard economic times, family members are expected to care for one another. The level of solidarity among Filipinos, their friendliness toward tourists and foreigners, and the ease with which one can find a polite stranger willing to help during a crisis are admirable at least and saintly at best. The Filipino congressmen we met proudly described not only the impressive outpouring of support from around the country after Typhoon Haiyan but also the aid sent from those Filipinos living abroad. Of all the places we visited during the Trek, the young scholars we worked with in the Philippines were the most deferential, respectful, and thankful for the opportunity to teach and learn alongside us.

The peoples of both Spain and the Philippines are spirited participants during *fiestas*. A festival of celebration, enjoyment, and camaraderie, the fiesta is one more cultural link between the Philippines and its Spanish heritage. During our time in Manila, I entered the elevator each morning to read an advertisement for the hotel's "buffet fiesta," and, weary with jet lag, I often felt as if I were back in Spain. There is little doubt that three hundred years in a Spanish convent has left a profound mark on the language, economy, and values of the Filipino society of the twenty-first century.

Fifty Years in Hollywood

Again one must ponder the question, "What's in a name?" According to a 2012 article in the *Philippine Star*, Mr. Carlos Pamintuan Celdran—our activist guide, who was once arrested for "offending religious feelings" while staging a protest inside Manila Cathedral—was christened Mr. John Charles Edward Celdran (Sauler, 2013). The article explains that his parents wanted him to have "an American-sounding name" in case they one day emigrated to the United States (Jarque, 2012). Although now he prefers to be called by the traditional Hispanic name Carlos, he contradicts other aspects of his Iberian-Catholic heritage by protesting the Church's abuses of power and its influence on the present Filipino government.

The story behind Mr. Celdran's original name and his current protests against the Church serve as an apt symbol of the transition from Spanish to American colonialism in the Philippines. From 1898 to 1946, the United States stripped away as much of the Spanish influence in the islands as it could, and during our week in Manila, I observed many ways in which America had succeeded in remolding the Philippines in its own Western, capitalist image (Celdran, 2015).

The United States acquired the Philippines from Spain after defeating the declining empire in the Spanish-American War in 1898. Even before the arrival of the Americans, the Filipino natives, led by Mr. Emilio Aguinaldo, had been rebelling against the Spanish, and when the American military, led by Admiral George Dewey, came to the Philippines to fight the Spanish, it promised that these native allies would be granted independence after the Spanish were defeated. But American President William McKinley altered his position during the peace negotiations with Spain. Recognizing that the Philippines would provide the U.S. with access to the large, untapped markets of Asia, and motivated by both economic imperialism and the racist values of the "White Man's Burden," McKinley "purchased" the Philippines from the Spanish and claimed the islands as U.S. property. America had finally acquired its first colony in Asia.

Three years of armed conflict between the native Filipinos and their new American rulers ensued before the population was "pacified" under the rule of Mr. William Howard Taft, who, as Governor, enacted a series of "pacification" laws that curbed civil liberties and forcibly suppressed rebellious sentiment (Francisco and Arriola, 1987). The U.S. Embassy in the Philippines contains hundreds of artifacts relating to this era in the nation's history. The building even boasts what one might call an "Imperialist Wall of Fame," with portraits of every Military Governor, Governor-General, and High Commissioner who served during the forty-eight years of American rule. On its website, the Embassy offers a host of facts, reports, and speeches related to the close economic and military relationship between the two nations. What cannot be found, however, are many references to Filipino history prior to American colonialism, nor to the outlawing and disappearance of such Spanish customs as the *siesta* (mid-day break) and *merienda* (afternoon snack).

The lasting legacies of American colonialism, like those of Spanish colonialism, are a mix of positive and negative. In order to understand the extent of the influence of U.S. colonialism on the Philippines, one need only turn again to the country's language. Dozens of terms in Tagalog are taken directly from English. Three words that we often encountered during our Trek indicate the nature of American influence: although Tagalog uses the Spanish-originating term *eko-nomiya* for the economy, the locals adopted the American term for the study of the economy—*ekonomiks*; the influence of consumerism and capitalism resulted in the adoption of *kodak* as a term for both camera and photograph; lastly, *titser*, the term for teacher, often came up during our discussions of the Americanization of the Filipino school system and the importance of English-language education for the national economy.

In their 1987 book *The History of the Burgis*, Ms. Mariel Francisco and Ms. Fe Maria Arriola argue that one of the most prominent and beneficial legacies of American rule in the Philippines has been the reformation of the country's education system and the adoption of English as a national language. The restructuring of the Filipino education system was not an act of altruism; rather it was part of the U.S. government's plan to pacify the rebel Filipinos and to "modernize" the islands in preparation for future self-governance. In the early twentieth century, the United States sent to the Philippines a naval ship, the *USS Thomas*, filled with American teachers, who became known as Thomascites. The teachers came armed with picture books and textbooks designed especially for the Filipino children, as well as modern products like toothpaste. As more and more young Filipinos received an American education, literacy rates and the dispersion of the English language rapidly increased across the archipelago (Francisco and Arriola, 1987).

This educational system had a major impact on the modern Filipino economy. Our Trek group attended a highly informative meeting at the Asia Institute of Management (AIM) in Manila with renowned Economics Professor Federico Macaranas. In his presentation, "Philippines and ASEAN: Exploring Policy Priorities for Asia's Sustainable Growth in the 21st Century," Dr. Macaranas cited the benefits that education and the English language have had on the Filipino economy. He listed English proficiency as one of the nation's top ten economic strengths. His presentation also contained a chart from the World Economic Forum ranking the Quality of Education Systems in meeting students' needs for a competitive economy. On a scale from 1 (not well) to 7 (extremely well), the study ranked the Philippines at 4.5, just behind its original model, the U.S. (4.6), and ahead of other, more "modern" nations like Japan (4.4), Korea (3.6), and Russia (3.5) (Schwab, 2014).

The English language and an American education system have also impacted the Filipino economy by influencing trends related to outsourcing and foreign remittances. Currently there is a major boom in call-center service, as American companies transition from India to the Philippines as the preferred hub for Business Process Outsourcing (BPO). According to *The Economist* (2012) and to the presentation we attended at AIM, "The Philippines overtook India in call-center business in 2011 and currently employs upward of 700,000 people with revenues of over 11 billion dollars. This revenue total amounts to just over five percent of its GDP." Professor Macaranas predicts that BPO from the United States will only continue to grow. He also argued that, as the Filipino higher education system improves, more technical sectors, including accounting and financial services, will be outsourced to the Philippines (Macarenas, 2015).

English-language skills have greatly enabled Filipino mobility, thereby fueling the brain drain and remittance trends. The Commission on Filipinos Overseas (2013) reported that over 3 million Filipino immigrants live in the United States alone. The same commission estimated that other English-speaking nations—Canada (759,000 Filipino immigrants), Australia (329,000), and the United Kingdom (160,000)—were the next most common destinations for permanent immigration among Filipinos. Remittances from this far-flung Filipino diaspora account for over ten percent of the Philippines' GDP (Macarenas, 2015). Thus the proliferation of the English language has had a lasting and beneficial effect on the Philippines' economy.

Once Filipinos acquired the English language, they also adopted many aspects of America's consumer-focused, capitalist culture. One indicator of this cultural influence is the presence of the aforementioned supermalls. A recent article by Professor Richard Heydarian (2015) in the *Huffington Post*, "Philippines' Shallow Capitalism: Westernization Without Prosperity," effectively explains the negative effects of this "Americanization." Indeed, he outlines issues that my fellow Trekkers and I observed during our visit: "Ordinary Filipinos boast about the astonishing fact that the Philippines—among the poorest countries in Asia—is home to three of the ten biggest shopping malls on earth… Shopping malls dominate—both physically and cognitively—the urban landscape of the Philippines" (Heydarian, 2015).

This rapid consumer movement is partly the result of the creation of a new middle class, comprising specifically those Filipinos recruited to work for American call centers. Unfortunately, the materialism pervading large parts of Filipino society has not relieved the painful income inequality between them and the vast working class, nor has it effected change in the rural, "semi-feudal" sectors of society (Heydarian, 2015). Instead, it demonstrates the negative consequences of the era of American rule in the Philippines. The U.S. colonial government severed some of the historically corrupt ties between the Catholic Church and the Filipino state, but the capitalist mentality that filled the power-vacuum left by the clergy has resulted in a system of crony-capitalism, which today's Filipino government has struggled to shake.

General MacArthur's "Return" and the Lasting Damage of World War II

"I shall return," General Douglas MacArthur said when the Philippines fell to the Japanese at the outset of America's entry into World War II. Many historians maintain that the U.S. lost the Philippines only because General MacArthur refused to follow military orders and attempted to combat an unexpected Japanese invasion with a squad of unprepared and ill-equipped soldiers. When General MacArthur was then forced to abandon the island, the Japanese slaughtered many of the American and Filipino troops left behind and forced the rest into labor camps. The most notorious instance of the Japanese army's cruelty at this time was the Bataan Death March, during which thousands of American POWs died. When the United States finally regained the upper hand in WWII, it was General MacArthur who elected to retake the Philippines, even though the islands were of little strategic importance at that point. Thus General MacArthur kept his word, but during his return he firebombed the Philippines to such an extent that Manila was no longer recognizable (Jose, 2010).

Knowledge of these events is imperative to understanding one overwhelmingly negative legacy of U.S. imperialism in the Philippines: the country's current infrastructure problems, especially with regard to transit, are remnants of the destruction of WWII and the subsequent rebuilding of the Philippines in the image of America in the 1950s.

During the Trek, I had the opportunity to interview CNN anchor Ms. Pia Hontiveros, the "Diane Sawyer" of Filipino news. Ms. Hontiveros echoed the argument, first presented to us in Professor Macaranas's presentation, that mass transit and infrastructure are among the biggest weaknesses in the Philippines. Although the nation has been moving up in many of the World Economic Forum's rankings, in transportation it still lags dramatically. Out of 142 participating nations, it ranks 113th in overall infrastructure quality, 100th in roads, 101st in railroads, 123rd in ports, 115th in airports, and 104th in electricity/energy (Schwab, 2014). The blame for these problems cannot be placed solely on American colonialism, as the corruption of Filipino politicians and technocrats have plagued the country as well, but, nevertheless, the destruction and bombing of Filipino cities by the U.S. and the lack of urban planning and funding following the war undoubtedly contributed to the Philippines' current struggles with transit and infrastructure.

The inadequate public transit and nightmarish traffic in Manila caused us many headaches during our visit. In other parts of Asia—Seoul, Bangkok, Hong Kong, and Guangzhou—we usually arrived early or on time for our many meetings and workshops. In Manila, by contrast, we were often late. Our hosts, however, were forgiving; they recognized that our late arrivals were due to the horrendous traffic. Because of a lack of public transit, the majority of Filipino people carpool to work in old, WWII-era American Humvees known as "jeepneys." These vehicles supposedly inherited this name because they look like military jeeps with people packed inside sitting "knee to knee." Interestingly, many jeepneys are decorated with stickers supporting American brands and sports teams.

Unsurprisingly, as a result of a shared language and similar consumption habits, there are many parallels between the cultural tastes of Americans and Filipinos. Filipinos love American films, hence the often-referenced phrase "fifty years in Hollywood." They also enjoy American fast food, music, brands, and sports. On the Trek, while driving around Manila, we saw many *basketbol* courts. We also noticed dozens of NBA basketball jerseys and jeepneys with NBA logos painted or decaled onto them. Such sights made us feel at home, but Ms. Francisco and Ms. Arriola, in *The History of the Burgis*, describe this "American colonial mentality" with a marked sting in the tail: "Americanization transformed consumption habits towards a preference for everything imported from the U.S. Symptoms of the colonial mentality in Filipino society include: Super Malls, imitation Louis Vuitton jeans, fake evergreen trees with cotton snow during Christmas, fashion magazines, [and] hoping the U.S. will intervene to solve our problems" (Francisco and Arriola, 1987).

Born and Raised in Asia

This essay has traced the influence of colonial "parenting" on the development of the Philippines. The nation's modern economy has certainly been shaped by its relationship with its two previous rulers. However, in order to fully understand the present-day Filipino economy, one must also take into account the archipelago's location in Asia. The Philippines has a long history with its neighboring Asian countries and especially with one of the region's preeminent powers, China. The profound influence of Chinese immigration on Filipino business and culture, as well as the threats and opportunities posed by the political and economic aspirations of modern China, will undoubtedly affect the Philippines' future.

"Out of the eleven Filipino billionaires in *Forbes* 2015 Richest Filipinos list, nine are Chinese-Filipino," reported the *Philippine Star* (Pedrosa, 2015). During our Trek, we spent several days learning from and working alongside one of these "chinoys" (the term often used to refer to Chinese-Filipinos)—Mr. Henry Sy, the CEO of a large conglomerate, the SM Group. Mr. Sy is worth an estimated 13.5 billion dollars, making him the richest man in the entire country. He was born in Southern China and immigrated to the Philippines in the 1930s at the age of twelve. Once there, he spent over a decade living and working in his father's convenience store, known as a *sari-sari* in Tagalog. After World War II, Mr. Sy began selling shoes, and eventually he opened up his first store, Shoemart (SM), in 1958 (SM History, 2015).

Over the next fifteen years, Shoemart expanded steadily. In 1972 Mr. Sy oversaw the construction and opening of the first SM department store in downtown Manila. Today the SM Group not only owns three of the ten biggest malls in the world but also manages Banco de Oro (BDO), the biggest bank in the Philippines; SM Cinema, the country's top movie-theater chain; and Tagaytay Highlands, the largest mountain resort. It has also become a national industry leader in a variety of other sectors, including housing development, biochemical manufacturing, and steel production (Flores, 2015). Alongside its business achievements, the SM group is a philanthropic leader in the Philippines. Through the SM Scholar Program, the company provides hundreds of Filipino youth from disadvantaged backgrounds with full tuition scholarships and monthly stipends. We were privileged to work with these industrious, intelligent, and generous SM scholars during our short time in Manila. One of them, Andy, deserves credit here for helping me with information for this essay.

In 2013 the Filipino Senate declared the Chinese New Year a "special working holiday as a sign of amity between the Philippines and China." In its declaration the government noted that just over one percent of the country's population (1.35 million) is ethnic Chinese and that a little more than twenty percent (22.8 million) have Chinese ancestry. Although Chinese-Filipinos are thus a relatively small percentage of the population, they are major players in the economy. A recent article in the *Philippine Star* reported that "Chinese-Filipinos control sixty percent of the private economy, about thirty-seven percent of banking equity, seventy-five percent of rice mills, forty percent of the lumber output, one-third of the one thousand largest corporations, and forty-seven out of sixty-eight public companies in the country" (Pedrosa, 2015).

The story of Chinese immigrants in the Philippines can be compared with that of the Jewish community in Europe. The Chinese, like their Jewish counterparts, were discriminated against, particularly during the Spanish and American colonial periods (Pedrosa, 2015). Under Spanish rule, the Chinese entered the marketplace in order to conduct trade with the affluent Spanish rulers, even though they faced "restrictive laws, expulsions, and occasional massacres" (Francisco and Arriola, 1987). When the United States took control, the government enforced the infamous Chinese Exclusion Act throughout the colony. This restrictive legislation was not repealed until 1943, just three years before the end of American rule. Despite the obstacles put before them, however, the Chinese persevered, creating an important role for themselves in Filipino society and succeeding even in the face of blatant discrimination.

Today "chinoys" are integral contributors to economic success in the Philippines, and yet some Filipinos have begun to worry about their political allegiance in light of an increasingly ambitious and unpredictable China. The most pressing issue putting strain on the relationship between China and the Philippines is the conflict over Chinese expansion in the South China Sea. Even the name of the Sea is controversial; many of the Filipinos we met referred to it as the "West Philippine Sea." In one meeting during our visit, representatives in the Ministry of Foreign Affairs outlined the legal case filed against China at The Hague. The Ministry showed us photos of Chinese naval-base development on what they consider to be part of the Philippines Archipelago and recounted stories of the Chinese navy expelling Filipino fishermen from national and international waters. Many analysts fear that the U.S. and its allies, especially Japan, may be pulled into a third World War if the tension between the Philippines and China in the South China Sea escalates into a full-scale conflict.

Entrepreneurs such as Mr. Henry Sy of SM and Mr. John Lim Gokongwei of JG Summit Holdings represent the impact of Chinese values on the economic and cultural development of the Philippines. Even the nation's hero and martyr for independence, Dr. Jose

Rizal, was a man with Chinese ancestry. The two nations share a long-standing partnership, but this friendship faces potential derailment thanks to their current territorial conflict. It is imperative that these two neighbors settle their claims in the South China and West Philippine Sea if they intend to continue to grow and prosper together.

The Future of the Halo-Halo Nation

The most famous Filipino dessert, halo-halo—Tagalog for "mix-mix"—is symbolic of what the Philippines has become, a nation known for its mixture of people, cultures, and styles (Celdran, 2015). Halo-halo includes a number of ingredients: shaved ice, evaporated milk, sweet beans, jellies, and fruit. Like Manila on a hot summer day, it can be very messy. But, similar to the Philippines and its people, halo-halo is also sweet, refreshing, and growing in international popularity. In 2013, the Filipino fast-food giant Jolibee opened a franchise in Los Angeles, and the halo-halo they served got rave reviews from renowned food critics such as Mr. Anthony Bourdain (Flores, 2013). Recent headlines, such as "The Philippines is Southeast Asia's new strong man" in *Bloomberg* (2015), indicate that the country is gaining recognition not only for its desserts but also for becoming an international, economic success story.

Both the Philippines' economy and its society have been strongly influenced by foreign powers. In this essay I outlined the impact of three hundred years in the Spanish convent, fifty years in Hollywood, three years of Japanese occupation and American military action during WWII, and a close geographical proximity to China. Besides those influences, there is the recent development of the high-powered

Filipino diaspora, which has cultivated strong ties with many countries in Europe, East Asia, and the Middle East.

Two relationships will be of the utmost importance for the Philippines in the near future. The first is a triangle, requiring the Philippines to balance its affairs with its former colonial parent, the United States, against its dealings with its ambitious neighbor, China. The current Filipino economic boom has been propelled, in large part, by business-process outsourcing from the United States. In order to continue growing at the current rate (5.6 percent in Q2 2015), the Philippines will need the United States to remain productive economically and to continue outsourcing business to the country. However, while the Philippines nurses its relationship with the U.S., it will also have to attend to the demands of China. In the press release announcing the Chinese New Year as a national holiday, the Filipino government highlighted its "flourishing relationship with China," mentioning China's place as the Philippines' third largest trade partner. But conflicts lurk behind this amicable tie. The South China Sea issue is a particularly powerful powder keg, one that could disrupt the triangular relationship among these three countries. The United States and the Philippines have a long-standing Mutual Defense Agreement and in 2014 signed a new "Enhanced Defense Cooperation Agreement," which obligates them to protect one another's interests. If the Philippines and China go to war over the disputed territories in the South China Sea, the U.S. would be pulled into the conflict and the dynamics of the region would change dramatically. On the other hand, if the Philippines and China settle their differences and continue to engage economically, the Philippines may have to distance itself from its former colonial parent.

The second important relationship in the Philippines' future development and growth is the relationship between the country's people and its leaders. The Philippines is no longer a colony ruled by a distant power, and neither is it a dictatorship under martial law, as it was for most of its post-independence life (1965-1986) under Ferdinand Marcos. Instead it is a young democracy beset by many of the problems that commonly inhibit young democracies, especially those of former colonies, such as extensive corruption and crony-capitalism. The Philippines remains highly unequal in its income disparities because the country's economy depends on oligopolies, in which a few large conglomerates and elite families control most of the major industries. The country's leaders are working tirelessly to solve the issues arising from this system—in our meeting with members of the Filipino House of Representatives, Speaker Feliciano Belmonte Jr. spoke of his high hopes for a newly passed anti-monopoly law—but the Philippines has gained notoriety for passing excellent legislation and then not being able to implement it successfully. Thus, although the Filipino economy has grown up fast and its future appears bright, its current leaders must find ways both to keep pace with the nation's economic development and to establish effective methods of legislative implementation. Only then will the halo-halo nation have a chance of succeeding as a stable and independent democracy in the long term.

Works Cited

"Asian Values." *The Economist*. The Economist Newspaper, 18 Apr. 2015. Web. 23 Sept. 2015.

"At the Front of the Back Office." *The Economist*. The Economist Newspaper, 23 June 2012. Web. Sept. 2015.

Celdran, Carlos. Personal Communication with the author. June 9, 2015. Chandran, Rina, and Sharon Chen. "Move Over Thailand, the Philippines Is Southeast Asia's Strong Man." *Bloomberg.com*. Bloomberg, 29 Jan. 2015. Web. Sept. 2015.

"Coming up Jasmine: Once a Laggard, the Economy of the Philippines Is Starting to Catch up." *The Economist*. The Economist Newspaper, 23 Aug. 2014. Web. Sept. 2015.

"Estimate of overseas Filipinos as of 2013." Commission on Filipinos Overseas. http://cfo.gov.ph/images/stories/pdf/StockEstimate2013.pdf

Flores, Wilson Lee. "Why Henry Sy Cried When He Saw His Father." *The Philippine Star*, 28 July 2010. Web. 23 Sept. 2015.

Francisco, Mariel N., and Fe Maria C. Arriola. *The History of the Burgis*. Quezon City: GCF, 1987. Print.

Heydarian, Richard Javad. "Philippines' Shallow Capitalism: Westernization Without Prosperity." *The Huffington Post*, 12 Jan. 2015. Web. Sept. 2015.

Jarque, Edu. "Carlos Celdran Walks - and Travels - His Way." *The Philippine Star*. N.p., 23 Sept. 2012. Web. Sept. 2015.

Litke, Mark. "Amid Population Explosion, Birth Control Access Roils the Philippines." *PBS Newshour*. PBS, 24 Aug. 2014. Web. Sept. 2015.

Marshall, Colin. "In Manila, Malls Aren't Passe – They Are the City Itself." The Guardian, 10 Dec. 2014. Web. Sept. 2015.

"Monsters Still, but Prettier." *The Economist*. The Economist Newspaper, 05 Jan. 2002. Web. 23 Sept. 2015.

Pedrosa, Carmen N. "Contribution of Chinese-Filipinos to the Country." *The Philippine Star*, 23 May 2015. Web. Sept. 2015.

Sauler, Ericka. "Celdran Found Guilty in 'Damaso" *The Inquirer*, 29 Jan. 2013. Web. Sept. 2015.

Schwab, Klaus. "Global Competitiveness Report 2014-15." World Economic Forum. http://www3.weforum.org/docs/WEF_GlobalCompetitivenessReport_2014-15.pdf

"Senate Declares Chinese New Year as Working Holiday." Senate of the Philippines: 16th Congress. Jan. 21, 2013. http://www.senate.gov.ph/press_release/2013/0121_prib1.asp

SM Shoemart History. SM Shoemart, n.d. Web. Sept. 2015. http://www.sm-shoemart.com/history.htm

Chapter 4

Entrepreneurship in India:

A Case Study of the Angul Coal-Gasification Steel Plant

Parul Batra

MBA, MIT Sloan School of Management

Bryant Renaud

MPP, Harvard Kennedy School of Government

● ●● ●

Introduction

After visiting Japan, South Korea, Indonesia, and Malaysia on the Asia Leadership Trek, we arrived at our fifth stop: India. India's growth story and the excitement around the newly formed government led by Prime Minister Modi featured in many of our discussions with leaders in other countries. When we arrived, the country was abuzz with preparations for President Obama's impending visit and meeting with Mr. Modi. We were excited to have the opportunity to learn more about India's plans for future growth and economic development from some of its most important business and government leaders.

Western media has discussed India's growth story for well over a decade. Its economic progression was slow under the left-leaning government for several decades. Then, in 1991, India took steps towards becoming a free-market economy and proceeded to grow at a much faster rate, due in part to economic liberalization reforms. In the 2000s, India's GDP grew at ~7-9 percent for more than a decade, driven by rapid growth in the services sector. In the early 2010s, however, India's GDP growth and FDI flow experienced a slump. The country's poor infrastructure, stringent labor laws, and overall difficulty in doing business (India was ranked #133 in the World Bank's rankings on the ease of doing business in 2010) scared away the once-attentive domestic and foreign investors. But recently, after the election of a new pro-business government led by Prime Minister Modi, India's GDP has once again started growing at a faster rate, and there is a new optimism globally about India's growth prospects in the coming decades.

Despite its rapid economic development, India is often criticized for not growing in an inclusive way. Critics point out that most of the country's recent economic development has been limited to the big urban centers, while people in the less-developed parts of the country continue to rely on traditional agricultural practices and live in poverty without access to high-quality healthcare, sanitation, and education. The inequality present in Indian society was evident to all of us on the Trek the minute we landed in the country and witnessed its high-rise glass buildings built next to slums and the young children begging outside shiny malls. This divide extends beyond economic lines. Despite his popularity, Mr. Modi is regarded with suspicion by

India's religious and other minorities, who worry that his conservative Hindu ideals and seemingly blind eye when it comes to mounting tensions will exacerbate ethno-religious divides.

Dr. Raghuram G. Rajan is the Governor of the Reserve Bank of India (RBI), and a major player in determining how India's economy is steered. When we met with Dr. Rajan in Mumbai, he illustrated the sheer scope of India's problem: it is no longer possible to follow the old growth path (first exporting textiles, then offering mass assemblies to industrial countries, and finally graduating to information economies). The industrial countries simply cannot provide the necessary demand.

If this worry seems too macro and abstract, consider a problem with concrete numbers: each year, twelve to fourteen million Indians join the workforce. In other words, a new Australia's worth of jobs is needed each year, if India is to keep people gainfully employed.

The economic and financial leaders of India thus face an array of challenges, among them figuring out how to develop domestic demand without slipping into inflation or a credit crunch; stimulating the creation of millions of jobs annually; and finding investors who will not drop ties at every social disruption. These tasks are some of the issues that keep Dr. Rajan up at night.

We also spoke in depth about India's strategy for fostering industry and business formation. The Governor warned us that India does not have a good track record in picking industries to bolster and that Mr. Modi's "made in India" campaign must focus on creating frameworks, infrastructure, human capital, and connectivity in order to succeed. It certainly must refrain from picking winners and losers by specific industry area.

Before closing, Dr. Rajan expressed concern for a topic that would reassert itself at several points during our trip: regulation. Land acquisition, protecting those with no paper deeds despite hundreds of years of habitation on a plot, and the strategic use of natural resources continue to be major concerns for Indians at the ground level all the way up to politicians in New Delhi.

With this background on India's economic development and income inequality, we were looking forward to understanding in more detail the country's growth plans for the coming years. Mr. Naveen Jindal is both the Chairman of Jindal Steel and Power Limited (JSPL), India's third-largest steel-producing company, and a former Member of Parliament. He is ideally positioned to reflect on India's recent political developments while also giving us his view about the private sector in India. Moreover, our meeting with Mr. Jindal involved visiting JSPL's coal gasification plant in Angul, a small district in the state of Odisha, which gave us an opportunity to visit a rural part of the country.

We were particularly excited to meet with Mr. Jindal and visit Angul because we had already heard about some of the political and regulatory hurdles JSPL had faced while setting up and operating the plant. We were also curious to hear about JSPL's sustainability initiatives, since it is one of the major steel- and power-producing companies in a country primarily reliant on coal for its energy needs and facing pressure from the global community to manage its carbon footprint. During our visit to the plant, we spoke extensively not only with Mr. Jindal but with Ms. Miniya Chatterji, Chief Sustainability Officer of JSPL, and Mr. Jona Pillay, Head of Jindal Coal Gasification Project, which enabled us to understand the many challenges that JSPL faced while setting up its coal gasification plant in Angul.

Our experience at the plant serves as an important case study of resource regulation, infrastructure development, sustainable technology, and the often disruptive impacts of altering the way factories and industries are established. It is the authors' hope that the study will be helpful to anyone wanting to learn more about setting up infrastructure projects in India and about the roles played by the government and the private sector in such investments—though we must also provide the caveat that this study presents only one view of the situation: our research was based entirely on our conversations with JSPL's employees mentioned above and does not include the views of other players in the situation, for example the government and the media, except by implication. Rather than provide a broad overview of all the players, this study focuses on one player in particular—JSPL itself—in order to provide a window into the intricacies of India's economic system.

The Angul Coal-Gasification Steel Plant

In mid-2000, Mr. Om Prakash Jindal (affectionately known as Mr. Babuji) was touring a Coal-To-Liquid fuel plant run by the company Sasol in Secunda, South Africa. The plant produced synthetic fuel (150,000 bbl/day of liquefied fuels) using a coal-liquefaction technology. Completed in 1980, in response to the embargo preventing the import of oil and natural gas to South Africa, the plant also produced a host of valuable by-products—town gas and downstream chemicals and fertilizers. Mr. Babuji was interested in using the same coal-gasification technology to make steel in his own country, India.

Mr. Babuji was the owner of a large steel and power company in India called the Jindal Group. At that time, Jindal Group was dependent on importing foreign coking coal to make steel using the conventional blast-furnace technique. He was tired of being exposed to the price variability of international coal markets for one of his plants' major inputs. He dreamt of making use of the enormous domestic coal reserves that India holds, but he knew that the type of coal found in India, non-coking, would never work for the blast-furnace methods currently in use. The coal-gasification technology at Sasol's Secunda plant, engineered by the German firm Lurgi GmbH, represented an opportunity to use entirely domestic resources—non-coking coal and iron ore—to make steel.

Fifteen years later, Mr. Babuji's son, Mr. Naveen Jindal—now Chairman of the company Jindal Steel and Power—faced a difficult decision: keep fighting for his father's vision of a more environmentally friendly steel plant that used indigenous coal as its feedstock, or submit to the mounting pressures that had been brought to bear against him and the plant's sustainability.

The Promise of Coal Gasification

Steel-making involves removing impurities from iron and combining it with other elements, such as nickel and vanadium. Steel-makers generally use two different methods to bring about this transformation. The first method is the basic oxygen method, which first uses an oxygen furnace to melt pig iron; then cooled oxygen and the other materials are used to remove impurities, prior to the alloy being introduced to the slag for final pouring. Though this approach is used in

Figure 1 The Lurgi Dry-Ash Gasifier

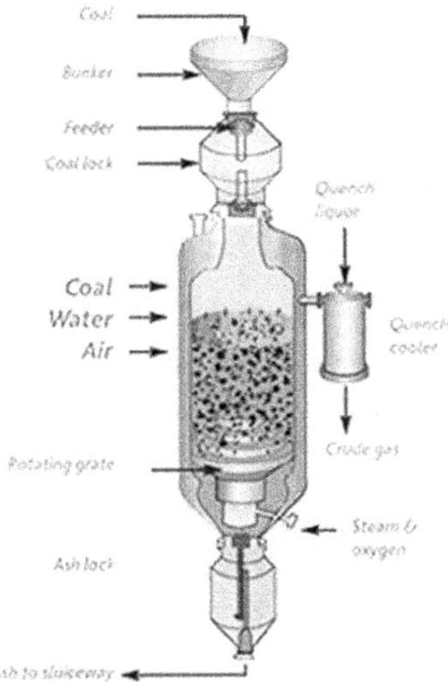

(http://www.netl.doe.gov/research/coal/energy-systems/gasification/gasifipedia/lurgi)

the majority of steel-production systems worldwide, the high capital costs of blast furnaces, coke ovens, and other factory units make it an endeavor with a high upfront cost. The second method is the electric arc furnace method. This requires a reduction gas, i.e. natural gas, to reduce solid ore in the direct reduction process , in order to produce "DRI." One major challenge for this approach is that natural gas is in short supply in India. As Secunda and others have proved, however, the reduction gas can also be derived from coal (specifically non-coking coal).

It was this last critical aspect—the possibility of deriving reduction gas from non-coking coal—that attracted Mr. Babuji and in turn his son Mr. Naveen to the coal-gasification technology used in South Africa.

While India's steel plants had heretofore relied on imported coking coal, which was necessary to run blast furnaces, a coal-gasification set-up would allow Jindal Steel & Power Limited (JSPL) to make use of locally available Indian non-coking coal, turning it into synthetic gas or syngas and in turn using the syngas as a reducing agent to make steel. Some by-products (e.g. tars, ammonia, and sulphur) also have potentially high market value.

Challenges in Building the Angul Plant

JSPL started construction of a DRI furnace and steel facility in 2009. The plant was sited in Angul, a small district in the state of Odisha, and strategically located less than five kilometers from a coal block. Developing all of the components on the same site and being able to transport coal from a nearby coal field would lead to greater efficiencies, larger profit margins, and a smaller environmental footprint.

JSPL acquired the coal block in Orissa in 2003, through the processes established by the government in 1993. The 1993 law enshrined the government's preference for awarding coal blocks to companies willing to perform value-add activities within India itself, instead of extracting the coal only to sell it in the international raw-materials market. With the proper permits in hand, JSPL started thinking about technology. In South Africa, Sasol had partnered with Lurgi, a German engineering and technology company, to set up Secunda CTL. Jindal followed the same model in India, engaging Lurgi to license out its gasifier technology to JSPL and to engineer several key processes critical to the plant.[1]

Lack of Domestic Technical Partners

Disaster struck in 2005, when Mr. O.P. Jindal died in a helicopter crash. His son, however, was just as determined to build the Angul plant. As the newly appointed Chairman of JSPL and a Member of the Indian Parliament representing the Congress Party, Mr. Naveen Jindal supported his father's focus on ensuring high-quality construction, as well as his insistence on partnering with domestic firms. Mr. Jindal knew that using domestic partners would result in a higher cost structure, but he was keen on developing Indian manufacturing know-how, just as he was keen on making good use of domestic coal resources. His approach was summed up as "Do it well, do it in-house." As a result of this decision, JSPL decided to use the Indian engineering firm, L&T, to manufacture its gasifier units.

Land Acquisition

Over the next few years JSPL carried out the painfully slow process of land acquisition—purchasing land from small-holders who lived where the future mine and plant sites would be located. Unlike in some countries with stronger eminent-domain policies, small-holders in India can resist selling for extended periods and thus interrupt the progress of large construction projects. The district of Angul, where some land needed to be cleared of forests and villagers, was no excep-

---

1   Gas cooling and cleaning, tar and phenol extraction, ammonia and Sulphur production, and the gasification process itself.

tion. JSPL made several efforts to give back to the local community, including paying salaries above market rate and engaging in efforts to provide community health and schooling, set up women's cooperatives, and employ locals. Despite these efforts, however, JSPL still had a hard time expediting the land-acquisition process.

Transporting Technology and Attracting Talent

In order to be close to a coal block and build a large plant on affordable and relatively unproductive land, JSPL planned to build the plant in a remote setting in the state of Odisha. But transporting large, heavy equipment and factory components out to the site was challenging and expensive. Vehicles with these loads had a hard time traveling on poor-quality roads and crossing dilapidated bridges.

The biggest challenge in building the plant was attracting and keeping talented workers and engineers on the remote Angul site. Since this was the first coal-gasification plant being built in India, the local engineers did not have the necessary know-how. JSPL recruited some of the best talent in the country, chemical engineers who had previous industry experience. It also recruited a small group of experienced South Africans who had worked on the Sasol plant. Yet, even after recruiting the right mix of people, retaining them remained a challenge.

Because of JSPL's diverse areas of expertise and the integrated nature of the plant, the engineers were able to make use of structural steel and cement directly from JSPL's own production, cutting down costs. Still, the project ran into difficulties in meeting deadlines and containing costs. Ultimately, building the world's first coal-gasification plant for DRI was completed several years late.

The Supreme Court Gets Involved

In 2012, the government's Comptroller Auditor General released a report that strongly affected JSPL's plans for operating the steel plant in Angul. The report concluded that, given average production costs, companies that had been awarded coal blocks over the preceding twenty years, since 1993, could be making as much as 295 Indian Rupees (about $5) in profit per ton of coal mined. The auditors then went on to estimate that these companies could make as much as $30 billion in aggregate profits over a thirty-year period. The report concluded that the government had lost billions in revenues because it had granted the licenses without competitive bidding; the report offered three recommendations for policy reform: (i) create a single window for permitting, (ii) use competitive bidding to ensure that the exchequer reaps a portion of the profits, and (iii) have the ministry of coal do more to incentivize good performance while punishing bad.

The media circulated this information rapidly and widely, portraying the current system as an unfair accruing of Indian people's money to private companies like JSPL. The comptroller's report itself did not mention anything about corruption, but the news reports elicited a flurry of accusations.

On September 24, 2014, JSPL weathered another blow when the Supreme Court of India declared that the land allocations made in the coal industry since 1993 were arbitrary and illegal, since they were conducted without competitive bidding. JSPL and other players in the industry were informed that 214 of the 218 blocks (including the Angul coal block) that had been allocated since 1993 would be de-allocated and reissued through a competitive bidding process. Furthermore, JSPL and other companies would have to pay an additional levy commensurate with the "excess" profits they had earned to date, which were 295 Indian Rupees per ton of coal extracted. The court also mandated that coal production must stop in these blocks by March 31, 2015.

These additional levies and redistributions would have a huge financial impact on the Angul plant. JSPL went along with the Government's decision and hoped that it would receive a fair chance at re-bidding for the Angul coal block. As promised, the government reallocated each of the 214 coal blocks towards either power production or iron/steel production. But the Angul coal block was delineated as a power-sector block, which implied that it could not be used by JSPL's Angul plant for steel production. JSPL filed a petition at Court against this decision, and the Court instructed the government to explain the basis of its allocation of the block. In February 2015, JSPL won back two of its other coal blocks in the bidding process. However, a few weeks later the government rejected JSPL's bids for the two blocks, citing them as "outliers" because they were lower than the winning bids for other, similar blocks. The government said that it would take a final decision on these mines only after further examination of the bidding process and prices and that it would consider the option of giving away these mines to either Coal India or the state governments.

For the coal-gasification technology to remain viable and operate sustainably, a captive coal block is quintessential. Coal at a higher price would make the technology financially unviable, ultimately impacting the entire process of steel-making. Also, the coal supply had to be close to the site, since the process requires that the coal be freshly mined and immediately gasified. A consistent supply of the same coal needs to be provided to avoid variation in the performance of the technology.

The Angul Plant Today

At the time of writing, the Angul plant runs at 50 percent capacity but is steadily ramping up; it is anticipated to reach 70 percent capacity over the next few months. The government's reversal of the bidding for the Angul coal block is currently under review in the Supreme Court of India. Even though the coal-gasification technology itself has proved to be more environmentally sustainable than other commonly used steel-manufacturing processes, its future in steel production depends on the decisions made by the Indian government and courts.

Sitting in his private plane en route to visit the Angul plant, Mr. Jindal set out for us the best- and worst-case scenarios. If JSPL wins the court case to re-designate the Angul coal block as a steel-production block, he will have the chance to bid for the block, hopefully win it, and then implement his plan of using Angul coal to make more environmentally-friendly steel. If the block remains designated for power, JSPL could still bid for it and use it to fuel one of its power plants nearby. However, this power plant is an 810 MW plant, costs $1 billion in investment, and has the potential to employ one thousand local workers. In comparison, the Angul steel plant is a $3+ billion investment and employs one thousand five hundred workers currently, a number that will probably increase as the plant reaches a higher capacity. Without the neighboring coal block, the Angul steel plant would need to bring coal from a greater distance, at a minimum of four times the cost. Moreover, coal bounces and grinds as it travels, which leads to more powder, or fines, that are unusable at the plant.

Mr. Naveen sighed, stared out the window, and wondered how he should proceed in order to make his father's vision of a more environmentally friendly steel plant come to life.

Conclusion

We believe that there is a lot to be learned from this case study about the roles that government and the private sector play in the economic development of a country. Our meetings with India's top businessmen and government leaders during the Asia Leadership Trek made it clear to us that India is at a critical juncture right now, with a high GDP growth rate, a favorable demographic dividend that will last for the next couple of decades, an educated and English-speaking workforce, rapidly increasing internet and mobile-phone penetration, and many other ingredients for economic success. History suggests that the private sector will play a dominant role in driving the country's economic development through job creation, workforce development, and investments in infrastructure and technology.

However, as highlighted by Dr. Rajan in our meeting with him, in order to maintain sustainable growth the government needs to provide necessary regulatory support and protection to the private sector and the country's citizens. While there is undoubtedly more complexity in this case than meets the eye, dilemmas like the one faced by JSPL have discouraged investment by private companies in India's less developed regions, especially among foreign investors who are less familiar with the country and more skittish in times of change. In order to attract investment, the government must do more to make the country business-friendly while maintaining a focus on pro-poor, inclusive growth.

The new government, led by Prime Minister Modi, is heavily focused on making India an easier place to do business; it has softened labor laws by making hiring and firing easier and liberalized key sectors to facilitate foreign investment. The administration also passed an ordinance whereby industry can acquire land from farmers more easily. Yet, while a lot of these business-friendly policy initiatives are well-intentioned, India has historically struggled with the implementation of such policies, due to rampant bribery and corruption in middle and lower layers of the government. Mr. Modi has discussed improving governance and transparency to eliminate corruption, a reform that, if successful, would help overcome the concerns around policy implementation over the next few years. Since our visit however, Modi's popularity seems to have dwindled. The ways in which his government reacts to the recent collapse of an industry-backed land reform bill, recovers from a much-criticized proposal to limit the RBI's monetary policy powers, and rises to critical social-policy challenges in the near future will play a large role in shaping India.

We feel fortunate to have had the opportunity to visit India on the Asia Leadership Trek and to learn about India from some of its top leaders at such an exciting and optimistic point in the country's history. We hope that as India strives for growth, the government will continue to prioritize social policies involving healthcare, education, and workforce training, in addition to promoting business-friendly policies.

Sources

http://www.icra.in/Files/ticker/Captive percent20Coal percent20Mining.pdf

http://www.netl.doe.gov/research/coal/energy-systems/gasification/gasifipedia/lurgi

http://www.tu-freiberg.de/~wwwiec/conference/conf07/pdf/4.1.pdf

http://www.jindalsteelpower.com/businesses/angul.html

http://en.wikipedia.org/wiki/Air_Liquide#Subsidiaries

http://en.wikipedia.org/wiki/Coal_gasification

http://en.wikipedia.org/wiki/Secunda_CTL

http://en.wikipedia.org/wiki/Steelmaking

http://inhome.rediff.com/money/2005/mar/31jindal.htm

http://www.sourcewatch.org/images/4/40/Draft_CAG_report_Pt_1.pdf

| Chapter 5 |

A Different Lens:
Comparing Race-Relations in Malaysia and the U.S.

Rachel Mason

Ed.M., Harvard Graduate School of Education

●●●

Introduction

As the first course of caviar and raw salmon diminished, so did our law-abiding conversation. "I'll have to speak softly," said Nur, my biracial Malay friend. "If the government officials at the next table hear me, I could be jailed or severely fined. We are not supposed to talk about these matters." The seventy-five-degree Malaysian summer weather did not fend off the icy shudder that traveled up my spine upon hearing Nur utter this statement.

I was seated with six other Asia Leadership Trek participants and the wife of the resort's world-renowned chef at a circular table cloaked in white linen at Banjaran Hotsprings Retreat in Ipoh, Malaysia. Moments earlier we had had the privilege of meeting the Founder and Chairman of Sunway Group at a cocktail reception—a calendar-worthy scene, complete with a natural hot spring enclosed by towering tropical mountains. The picturesque setting, coupled with the glass (or two) of white wine I had just consumed, contributed to my floating-on-cloud-nine feeling. Consequently, I was visibly jarred when Nur made the unfathomable claim that she could be imprisoned for her upcoming comments.

Prior to my visit to Malaysia, I had been unfamiliar with the country's racial dynamics. That night at the Banjaran Hotsprings Retreat not only piqued my curiosity but illuminated my lack of knowledge about Malaysia's racial history. As a Human Development and Psychology Ed.M. candidate at the Harvard Graduate School of Education, I was especially interested in the origin of Malaysia's institutionalized racial discrimination and the effects of such racism on the targeted population, especially youth. After that night I pursued the topic by observing Malaysian culture, interacting with youth in Malaysia, and researching the scholarly literature on Malaysian race relations. Comparing what I discovered with my own race-related narrative, I investigated Malaysia's historical and current racial situation while identifying parallels to race relations in the United States.

As she enjoyed five-star cuisine just an arm's length away from some of Malaysia's most influential political and business figures, Nur courageously explained the three main racial groups in Malaysia: Malays constitute approximately 66 percent of the country's population, Malaysian Chinese 26 percent, and Indians 8 percent (Kuppusamy, 2006). Malaysia's social hierarchy corresponds with the racial percentages: Malays are ranked the highest, followed by Malaysian Chinese, and then Indians. Native Malays, known in Malaysia as *bumiputera*, are the most privileged ethnic group; the government has given them explicit and exclusive rights and privileges, including educational priority, private affordable housing, lower interest rates, and the determination of the national religion, which is, accordingly, Islam. The higher status of the Malaysian-Chinese population over the Indian population is evident in the naming of these ethnic groups. While neither the Chinese nor the Indian residents are native to Malaysia, the Chinese population has been granted a form of acceptance in their name of "Malaysian Chinese," while the Indian population is referred to not as "Malaysian Indian" but solely as "Indian."

An Overview of Malaysia's Racial History

In order to appreciate Nur's perspectives on Malaysia's current racial situation, one must understand the country's tumultuous racial history. The late 1880s marked the beginning of the three racial groups' coexistence. Malaysia, then part of the British Empire, was suffering from an insufficient labor force (Yacob, 2006). The British government recruited Chinese and Indian laborers to work in the Malaysian tin mines and rubber industries respectively; but the government deliberately segregated the immigrants from each other and from the native Malay, or *bumiputera*, population. The separation of races was "reinforced in the premeditated colonial policy of maintaining a division of labour along ethnic lines," so "there were very few opportunities for members of the three racial groups" to interact (Yacob, 2006). When Malaysia gained independence from the British in 1957, nearly seventy years after the first Chinese and Indian laborers had arrived, the majority of Malaysia's Indian and Chinese populations "still maintained their political allegiance to their respective home countries" (Yacob, 2006).

After Malaysia's independence from Britain, the Malaysian government acknowledged the need for "political trust among the three social groups and the abolishment of the social paranoia that characterizes fragmented culture" in order to promote a peaceful society (Yacob, 2006). However, the "sudden…shift from the pre-war policies only caused political disorientation among the people who had adapted to the earlier imposed segregations" (Yacob, 2006). The Malaysian Chinese and Indian population were focused on reestablishing their life in the post-war economic reconstruction, while the Malay population greeted the government's plan of swift unity with hostile rejection (Yacob, 2006). The sharp division of wealth between the urban-dwelling Chinese and the poor rural Malays added to the country's mounting tension (Chua, 2012).

Months prior to the enactment of independence from Britain, the Reid Commission—an independent commission composed of both Malays and British administrators—was established, with the directive of drafting a new Malaysian Constitution. The result was the Report of the Federation of Malaya Constitutional Commission 1957, or The Reid Commission Report, which prioritized the "safeguarding" of Malay privileges. The Chief Minister at the time realized the consequences of bestowing privileges solely upon one racial population. He stated, "in an independent Malaya all nationals should be accorded equal rights, privileges and opportunities and there must not be discrimination on grounds of race and creed" (Reid Commission Report, 1957). Despite the Chief Minister's warning, however, the Report outlined four exclusive Malay privileges, which had first been made explicit in the Federation Agreement of 1948. The four matters in which "the special position of the Malays is recognized and safeguarded," as stated in the Report, are as follows:

1 In most of the States there are extensive Malay reservations of land, and the system of reserving land for Malays has been in operation for many years. In every State the Ruler-in-Council has the power to permit a non-Malay to acquire a piece of land in a Malay reservation but the power is not used very freely. There have been some extensions of reservations in recent years but we do not know to what extent the proportion of reserved land has been increasing.

2 There are now in operation quotas for admission to the public services. These quotas do not apply to all services, e.g., there is no quota for the police and, indeed, there is difficulty in getting a sufficient proportion of non-Malays to join the police. Until 1953 admission to the Malayan Civil Service was only open to British subjects of European descent and to Malays but since that date there has been provision for one-fifth of the entrants being selected from other communities. In other services in which a quota exists the rule generally is that not more than one-quarter of new entrants should be non-Malays.

3 There are also in operation quotas in respect of the issuing of permits or licenses for the operation of certain business-es. These are chiefly concerned with road haulage and

passenger vehicles for hire. Some of these quotas are of recent introduction. The main reasons for them appear to be that in the past the Malays have lacked capital and have tended to remain on the land and not to take a large part in business, and that this is one method of encouraging the Malays to take a larger part in business enterprises.

4 In many classes of scholarships, bursaries and other forms of aid for educational purposes preference is given to Malays. The reason for this appears to be that in the past higher education of the Malays has tended to fall behind that of the Chinese, partly because the Chinese have been better able to pay for it and partly because it is more difficult to arrange higher education for Malays in the country than for Chinese in the towns.

Although members of the Malaysian government denounced the unequal treatment of Malaysian residents in 1948 and again in 1969, many of these privileges are still being upheld as legally legitimate today, in Malaysia's current society.

May 13, 1969, the day of the 1969 Race Riots in Kuala Lumpur, was one of the most monumental days in Malaysia's history. Debates still arise over the exact causes, happenings, and number of deaths and injuries. The Malaysian government supports the theory that the riots occurred solely for political reasons: "the riots were sparked by opposition parties 'infiltrated by communist insurgents' following huge opposition gains in the election" (Kuppusamy, 2006). The truth seems to be more closely tied to racial tensions: in the general election on May 10th, 1969, the UMNO (United Malays National Organization) "retained an overall majority [but]…lost its two thirds majority, and its control of Selangor state was threatened" (Kuppusamy, 2006). The Malays' political dominance was now threatened, as a result of the predominantly Chinese opposition party's success in the election. The resulting riots indicate the extent to which racial tension was spurring the conflict: 196 people were killed, according to the disputed Malaysian police figures (Kuppusamy, 2006); these figures state that 143 of those killed were Chinese, twenty-five were Malay, thirteen were Indian, and fifteen were individuals of undetermined ethnicity (Von Vorys, 2015). Contemporary Western diplomatic sources estimated the Chinese-Malaysian death toll to be six hundred (*Time*, 1969), while first-hand observers and correspondents argued that a four-figure death toll was more likely (Slimming, 1969). Malaysian official figures state that an additional "439 individuals were injured, 753 cases of arson were logged, and 211 vehicles were destroyed or severely damaged" (Funston, 1980).

As a result of the riots, the government declared a state of national emergency. The national parliament was replaced until 1971 by the National Operations Council (NOC), whose mission was to restore law and order in Malaysia. According to Mr. Karl Von Vorys, the October 9th, 1969 report released by the NOC "cited 'racial politics' as the primary cause of the riots, but was reluctant to assign blame to the Malays" (Von Vorys, 2015). The report states:

> The Malays, who already felt excluded in the country's economic life, now began to feel a threat in their place in the public services. No mention was ever made by non-Malay

politicians of the almost closed-door attitude to the Malays by non-Malays in large sections of the private sector in this country.

In 1971, the Malaysian Government implemented the New Economic Policy (NEP), declaring that its mission was "To reduce and eradicate absolute poverty irrespective of race through raising income levels and increasing employment opportunities for all Malaysians; and To restructure society to correct economic imbalances so as to reduce and eventually eliminate the identification of race with economic function" (New Economic Policy, 2013). While the initial intent of the NEP was to promote social harmony and economic equality, the efforts to alleviate poverty mainly focused on eradicating the still-present income gap between the Malays and the Chinese population (Kuppusamy, 2006). Consequently, the existence of special privileges for the Malays persisted, and legal racial discrimination against the non-Malay population increased. "In a bid to maintain social order, [Prime Minster] Mahathir often blacked out foreign news coverage when racial tensions erupted in nearby Indonesia, where the Chinese are also a minority population" (Kuppusamy, 2006). Originally designed to end in 1991, The New Economic Policy of 1971 has gone uninterrupted by government intervention and continues to this day (Kuppusamy, 2006).

In an effort to gauge the racial and social climate of Malaysia, the first wide-scale survey of race relations in more than fifty years was conducted in the early 2000s. The data of nearly one thousand two hundred Malaysian residents indicates that the country's three main racial populations live peaceful yet separate lives, as most of the residents seek comfort and security with those in their respective ethnicity (Kuppusamy, 2006). According to the survey, "Only 11 percent of the respondents said they had eaten often with friends from other races in the previous three months, and 34 percent said they had never had a meal with people of other races" (Kuppusamy, 2006). Lawyer and senior leader of the opposition party Mr. A. Sivanesan stated, "Half a century after independence we are further away from knowing each other than when we started—separate schools, separate friends, separate lives" (Kuppusamy, 2006). These results are in direct opposition to the Malaysian's government attempt to promote their country as having a common "Malaysian" identity; in reality the government's claim of unity is grossly inaccurate. In contrast, Mr. Sivanesan believes that "all Malaysian political parties that restrict membership on grounds of race, religion or sex" should be eradicated (Kuppusamy, 2006).

The colonial roots of racial segregation and inequality in Malaysia certainly laid the groundwork for today's clear lines of division, but legal support and cultural norms now reinforce them on a daily basis. Remembering one form of inequality—the initial income-gap between the Malaysian Chinese and the Malays after independence—the Malaysian government has prolonged inequality of another kind, through institutionalizing the privileges of Malays over the country's other racial populations.

Nur's Biracial Malaysian Experience

In order to gain a more in-depth first-hand account of Malaysia's current state of racial affairs, I interviewed Nur, who is a life-long

Malaysian resident, in a private setting. Nur's comprehensive narrative confirmed that there is rampant racism in Malaysia. She said that the Chinese are the wealthiest racial group and that the Indians are the lowest on the socioeconomic scale, lacking both the wealth of the Chinese and the government protection of the Malays. She listed the privileges afforded to the Malays, including political dominance, lower interest rates on significant monetary investments, and access to exclusive real estate. Interestingly, she argued that determining the country's instituted religion and receiving superior educational access and support are the two most influential entitlements granted to the Malay population, as these factors influence nearly every facet of daily life.

Nur's parents dated for ten years before they got married because her paternal grandmother was against her parents' union, on the grounds of their differing religions. While Nur is one-eighth Malay and seven-eighths Chinese, her parents gave her a traditional Muslim Malay name. Because the national religion is Islam, by law all Malays must have Muslim names—a regulation that also requires all Malay women's names to include Binti, meaning female, and all Malay men's names to include Bin, meaning male.

Nur's elementary-school years marked her first vivid understanding of personally directed racism. Nur was unique among her classmates: her fair skin and large, almond-shaped eyes contrasted with her Muslim name. Her Malay classmates shunned her because they thought she looked Chinese, and her few Chinese classmates excluded her because she did not speak Mandarin, only Malay and English. Therefore, Nur mostly spent time with Indian students, who also experienced exclusion as the lowest members of the Malaysian social hierarchy.

When Nur was seven years old, she was playing at recess with her only friend, an Indian classmate, when the girl's older sister approached them, aggressively pulled her sister away, and screamed, "What are you doing with this girl? Don't you see she isn't our kind? You should be careful." The girl defended Nur, and their friendship continued, but the incident remained in Nur's memory. Her elementary-school experiences expose the flaw in the Malaysian government's claim of one "Malaysian" identity; it is evident that, even from a young age, Malays and non-Malays are encouraged to stick to their own racial groups. Nur's ostracism demonstrates the detrimental effects of Malaysia's widely held racial beliefs and the constant reiteration of prejudice, which extends even to the youngest, most malleable minds.

From the ages of thirteen to seventeen, Nur attended a high school that accepted only Muslim Malay students. Nur was the sole "Chinese" student, accepted on the basis of her one-eighth Malay heritage, and she found it difficult to create true friendships; consequently, she continued to be socially isolated. She channeled her energy into academic success, but despite her exceptional grades, she was still denied acceptance into the top Malaysian universities, since Malays invariably receive top priority.

Many of Nur's Malaysian-Chinese and Indian peers have begun to seek higher education in foreign, especially European, countries, rather than endure exclusion from Malaysia's top universities. The outflux of these young, bright students is a leading cause of Malaysia's current economic stagnation, for a majority of them then pursue careers aboard, depriving their native country of their creative and entrepreneurial efforts. Their departure is just one of the many ways in which the pervasive racial inequality in Malaysia, institutionalized in the laws and reinforced in the attitudes of the population—even the attitudes of its children and young students—is damaging the country.

A Comparison between Malaysia and the U.S.

Initially I was flabbergasted by Nur's stories and by my own investigation into Malaysia's racial history. Soon, however, I began to see parallels with my own experience in America. Like Nur, I am biracial. My blonde-haired, blue-eyed mother is white, and my freckled, curly-haired father was African-American. While Nur's upbringing in Malaysia and my own in the United States were of course different in many ways, we still share similar core values, which in part stem from our biracial backgrounds.

Nur and I each grew up in a country where the two races to which we belong were historically, and currently, in opposition with each other. We navigated disturbing biases on both sides in school, the media, and among our friends, while hearing varying accounts of the situation from our parents and extended family. Yet, with help from supportive family members and friends, Nur and I were both able to turn these challenges to our advantage: we learned to process the many different opinions, facts, and views that bombarded us and to develop our own perspectives, while remaining open to new ways of expanding our racial understanding. As a result, we are both open-minded and have the ability to assess situations with a critical but sympathetic eye.

For me, this gift of being open-minded and curious extends beyond race-related situations, allowing me to understand individuals in every arena. Thanks to my upbringing and appearance, I feel able to connect with people from all walks of life, regardless of how different they are from me. I've also learned, through my own experience of difference, to acknowledge the similarities in human thought and behavior, for good or ill. Prejudice looks familiar no matter where it arises, and I have found many parallels between the race-related laws, policies, and practices of Malaysia and those of the U.S.

It was due to the 1880s labor shortage in Malaysia that Malays, Chinese, and Indians were first brought together in Malaysia. Labor shortage was also the main reason that the first Africans were brought forcibly to Jamestown in 1619. It is unclear whether the imported Africans were considered "indentured servants" or slaves at this time, but, in any case, they were viewed as a valuable free labor source, and forty years later, in 1662, laws passed that officially deemed slavery legal in Jamestown (National Park Services, 2015). Prejudice against Africans, slaves, and dark complexions permeated the privileged white population, ensuring the preservation of their high social status. The non-white population were deprived of stable familial structures, marriage, a sense of community, religious freedom, and just work compensation. While, in Malaysia, the Chinese and Indians were not subjected to such inhumane discrimination, the privileged Malay population, like the white population in Jamestown, received (and still receives) exclusive benefits, rights, and protection.

Mr. S. Yacob's argument about the separation of races in Malaysia—that it was "reinforced in the premeditated colonial policy of maintaining a division of labour along ethnic lines," so "there were very few opportunities for members of the three racial groups" to interact, divisions that created "social paranoia" and a "fragmented culture" long after the country's independence in 1957 (Yacob, 2006)—could also apply to the racial situation in the United States. America's Civil War, from 1859 to 1865, sparked the government's enactment of official racial equality, but, as in Malaysia, the "sudden…shift from the pre-war policies only caused political disorientation among the people who had adapted to the earlier imposed segregations" (Yacob, 2006). The U.S. government's "plan of effortless and swift unity was met with resistance," as the black population focused on "post-war economic reconstruction," while a majority of the white population "met the concept of [racial equality] with hostile rejection" (Yacob, 2006).

Moreover, similarly to Malaysia, the unity of the races was not truly desired by the American government. The 13th Amendment of the U.S. Constitution, ratified in 1865, abolished slavery in America: "Neither slavery nor involuntary servitude, except as a punishment for crime whereof the party shall have been duly convicted, shall exist within the United States, or any place subject to their jurisdiction" (National Archives, Record 11). However, as the Malaysian government strove to preserve the special privileges of the Malay population, so did many members of the U.S. government—especially those in the South—strive to preserve the privileged social and economical status of the white population. Hence the introduction in 1865 of the Black Codes, the South's attempt to retain white rule and restore slavery. These codes varied from state to state in the South, but they were alike in prohibiting blacks from bearing arms, voting, marrying whites, and learning how to read and write. The Black Codes applied to all non-whites but were directed primarily at people of African descent: South Carolina's code, for example, applied to "persons of color," which was defined as including anyone with more than one-eighth Negro blood (urt-usa, 2015). While the Black Codes were often more explicitly discriminatory than Malaysia's New Economic Policy a century later, both policies demonstrate that the two countries' governments were not truly seeking a racially equal and inclusive society.

In both the U.S. and Malaysia, racially fueled riots and injustices have occurred, both prior to the "equality acts" and currently. Tensions arose prior to the Malaysian Race Riots of 1969 because the Chinese political party's victory in the election threatened the Malay party's dominance, and the tense atmosphere was electrified when a Chinese youth was shot and killed by Malay police in Kuala Lumpur (Ness, 1972). This shooting of an unarmed, racial-minority youth by a racially privileged law-enforcement official seems especially pertinent in a comparison with today's America, given the recent shootings in the U.S. of unarmed black youth by white police officers. The government-controlled Malaysian media purposefully portrayed the Chinese population in a negative light following the 1969 Race Riots, withholding crucial facts about the causes of the riots and the actual Chinese death toll (*Time*, 1969). Similarly, the American media's portrayal of the black community following the events at Ferguson and other shootings emphasized violence, disruption, and chaos. Peaceful, self-organized youth groups and protests were not shown on mainstream U.S. media, while the perspectives of the police and government officials were heavily broadcast: "News reports often headline claims from police or other officials that appear unsympathetic or dismissive of black victims" (Wing, 2014). As the philosopher Mr. Paulo Friere stated in 1970, "Never in the history of humanity has violence been initiated by the oppressed; structural violence does not occur without oppression" (Freire, 1970).

The current segregation of racial populations in Malaysia, as demonstrated in the wide-ranging 2006 survey gauging the country's racial climate, also has parallels in the U.S. Racial homogeneity can be seen in a majority of U.S. residential, educational, and occupational venues. In a Deloitte report last year on HR trends, "Diversity/Inclusion was consistently reported as one of the least important issues on leaders' minds compared to other HR matters" (Rezvani, 2015). Additionally, "a full one-fifth of respondents indicated their organizations have very informal diversity efforts with nothing structured at all, with 41 percent of study respondents specifying the underlying reason being that they're 'too busy'" (Rezvani, 2015). In educational institutions, "the historical record demonstrates that residential segregation is *de jure*, resulting from racially-motivated and explicit public policy whose effects endure to the present" (Rothstein, 2014). Some change is being attempted: housing desegregation has now been deemed a constitutional necessity, and rectifying this matter would alter "policies like voiding exclusionary zoning, placing scattered low and moderate income housing in predominantly white suburbs, prohibiting landlord discrimination against housing voucher holders, and ending federal subsidies for communities that fail to reverse policies that led to racial exclusion" (Rothstein, 2014). Nevertheless, despite such efforts to rectify cultural segregation, the portrayal of America as a "melting pot," an image implying a complete lack of divisions, is far from accurate.

The continuance of residential and professional racial divisions has resulted in a continuance of racial homogeneity. The *Loving v. Virginia* Supreme Court case eradicated the prohibition of interracial marriages in 1967, but it was only in 2000, thirty-three years later, that the Census allowed respondents to identify as belonging to multiple races (CensusScope, 2000). In 2000 the percentage of Americans who self-identified as multiracial was 2.4 percent (CensusScope, 2000). Proximity is one of the key factors influencing an individual's choice of mate, and because of the predominantly homogenous residential, educational, and occupational institutions in the U.S., this proximity is limited for most Americans. The lack of racial diversity can also be seen in both the American and Malaysian governments. Mr. Barack Obama, sworn in as America's forty-fourth president in 2009, is the country's first president not to be fully white; his appointment was remarkable in part because of the rarity of non-white people in American politics.

Even though the blatant discriminatory laws of Malaysia do not have exact parallels in America, structural racism still thrives in this nation known for its promise of equality. A recent survey found that American job applicants with Anglo-Saxon surnames are 50 percent more likely to receive a response from a potential employer than applicants with African-American surnames, even when their resumes are nearly identical (Francis, 2003).The level of discrimination was statistically uniform "across all the occupation and industry categories covered in the experiment" (Francis, 2003). The majority of the white population also has access to better education at every stage of childhood and youth, and upon completion of schooling, they are more likely to attain a high-paying occupation (Bidwell, 2013). Their higher income affords them the privilege of living in safer neighborhoods and raising children who will be better protected by law-enforcement officials (Bradner, 2013). These children, brought up in safety and comfort, will also have access to superior education, and so the cycle continues. Such structural discrimination calls to mind Nur's experience of Malaysia's unequal system of university admittance, when her exceptional academic performance was effectively canceled out by government-imposed racial quotas. These examples of institutionalized racism discredit the governments of both Malaysia and America and contradict the idea that one can refer to a unified "Malaysian" or "American" identity.

The most striking difference between the two countries is of course that Malaysia's racism is still explicitly condoned by law. Removing discriminatory laws would not eliminate all the culturally ingrained racism—as seen in the parallel case of America—but it would still be a crucial step forward.

I believe, however, that the key to a more peaceful and inclusive Malaysian society, beyond the obvious need for eliminating its discriminatory laws, is to address the root cause of racial discrimination and the resulting income discrepancies. Discrimination arises from the widely held belief that people's skin color, social status, and income levels dictate their worth and the way they should be treated. These prejudices are cultural as well as political, and in both Malaysia and the U.S. they have become so deeply imbedded that they are passed on from generation to generation.

As a biracial American, I live in a duality, connected with both the racial oppressors and the racially oppressed. Yet, from my own experiences, I have learned that referring to "oppressors" and "oppressed" compounds the problem. Because racial inequalities so often arise from complex historical events, as seen in both Malaysia and America, it is important not simply to blame the privileged races: in the words of the British philosopher James Allen, "Both oppressor and those who are oppressed are cooperating in ignorance, and while seeming to afflict each other, are in reality afflicting themselves" (Allen, 1998). To reach a harmonious society, one must neither condemn the racial oppressors nor praise the racially oppressed but instead compassionately embrace both. Such an attitude requires a fundamental shift in mindset, and thus Malaysia's remedial measures need to offer more than external integration. Such efforts may temporarily create "diverse" environments, but diverse environments are futile if the underlying biases remain to prevent the creation of authentic, respectful, and loving interpersonal relationships. Instead, Malaysia's educational system should emphasize self-awareness and the understanding of others. Individuals in each of the nation's three racial groups should learn to value their own cultures without dismissing those of others. Undoubtedly, cultural differences exist, and those differences should be respected and explored; but the political and institutional emphasis in any country should be on inclusion and equality. Only then can every individual gain true freedom.

Conclusion

In February of 1991, the Malaysian Prime Minister at the time, Dr. Mahathir bin Mohamad, stated in his speech on "Malaysia: Vision of the Future":

But I do believe that the narrowing of the ethnic income gap, through the legitimate provision of opportunities, through a closer parity of social services and infrastructure, through the development of the appropriate economic cultures, and through full human resource development, is both necessary and desirable. We must aspire by the year 2020 to reach a stage where no one can say that a particular ethnic group is inherently economically backward and another is economically inherently advanced. Such a situation is what we must work for—efficiently, effectively, with fairness and with dedication.

The Prime Minister claimed that a more economically "equitable society" was "both necessary and desirable," yet he also argued that "we must ensure the healthy development of a viable and robust *Bumiputera* commercial and industrial community" (Mohamad, 1991). In contrast, former Malaysian Deputy Prime Minister Anwar Ibrahim stated, "We need to appeal to the Malays, Chinese and the Indians and the rest that we need to go beyond race-based politics. If you continue to harp on and support this racial equation, you will never be able to overcome racial divisions" (Kuppusamy, 2006). Ibrahim's proposition "to reform the political landscape, which…is straining national harmony," was not protected by the government, and he was jailed in 1998 for his views (Kuppusamy, 2006). How will an equitable society arise if the leaders of the country are not truly invested in its attainment, and if those who speak out in support of equality are imprisoned as a result?

While I did not directly ask Nur what she believes should be done to improve the current state of race relations in Malaysia, our interview revealed her frustration with the lack of equality and of freedom of choice in Malaysia. Equal educational opportunities and religious freedom would have alleviated numerous issues for Nur: the state-imposed rules governing both educational and religious practices have drastically affected her life, in everything from her personal appearance to her romantic life to her private conversations.

Yet, even if the Malaysian government were to embrace equality in its policies, initiatives for equal educational access may not be enough. Recently the Malaysian government implemented racial-integration programs in schools. In the Vision School, "students share sports fields, assembly halls and canteens, but attend classes conducted in their own languages… But the initiative is embroiled in controversy, mainly because of the fear among Chinese and Indians that the vernacular education system would suffer and erode their ethnic identities" (Kuppusamy, 2006). The reluctance of the Chinese and Indian students to embrace the system, despite the fact that it is was put in place primarily to benefit them, demonstrates the complexity of the issue and the difficulty of promoting integration while simultaneously respecting the unique customs of each culture. Another attempt to integrate students is the Malaysian national-service program, begun in 2004, which "puts youths of all races under a single roof. Students are chosen at random and taken to camps for about three months in the hope that they will learn teamwork and absorb one another's cultures" (Kuppusamy, 2006). However, due to the deeply entrenched racial beliefs of both the children and their parents, experts say these "halfhearted measures" are unlikely to create a culture of greater equality (Kuppusamy, 2006).

Ultimately, the Malaysian government needs first and foremost to eradicate its discriminatory laws and practices. All the loopholes that still give privileges to the select few must be closed. But, in the aftermath of the discriminatory-law removal, it will be crucial to find active and effective ways, through education and the public promotion of tolerance, to preserve the unique cultural traditions of the Malay, Malay-Chinese, and Indian populations while at the same time encouraging openness and interaction among the races. The goal would not be to eliminate all the differences between the three racial groups, but rather for all individuals to be afforded equality and free choice in every aspect of their lives. Only when people like Nur can go to the universities they deserve, practice the religious beliefs they prefer, engage in relationships with individuals of any race, and talk freely in public places will Malaysia be able to claim that it offers equality to all races.

Works Cited

Allen, J., & Allen, M. (1998). *As You Think*. Novato, Calif.: New World Library.

Adam, Ramlah binti, Samuri, Abdul Hakim bin & Fadzil, Muslimin bin (2004). *Sejarah Tingkatan 3*. Dewan Bahasa dan Pustaka.

African Americans at Jamestown. (2015, June 20). National Park Services. Retrieved June 25, 2015, from http://www.nps.gov/jame/learn/historyculture/african-americans-at-jamestown.htm.

Bidwell, A. (2013, July 31). "Report: Higher Education Creates 'White Racial Privilege.'" *U.S. News*.

Bradner, E. (2014, December 3). "Fact check: Grim statistics on race and police killings." Retrieved August 21, 2015.

CensusScope. "Multiracial profile." (2000). Retrieved 2015, from http://www.censusscope.org/us/s2/chart_multi.html

Francis, D. (2003). "Employers' Replies to Racial Names." Retrieved August 21, 2015, from http://www.nber.org/digest/sep03/w9873.html

Freire, Paulo. *Pedagogy of the Oppressed*. New York: Herder and Herder, 1970.

Gayl D. Ness (May 1972). "REVIEW: *May 13: Before and After*, by Tunku Abdul Rahman; *Malaysia: Death of a Democracy*, by John Slimming; *The May 13 Tragedy: A Report*, by The National Operations Council; *The May Thirteenth Incident and Democracy in Malaysia*, by Goh Cheng Tiek." *The Journal of Asian Studies* 31 (3): 734–736. doi:10.1017/s0021911800137969.

John Funston (1980). *Malay Politics in Malaysia: A Study of the United Malays National Organisation and Party Islam*. Heinemann Educational Books (Asia).

John Slimming (1969). *The Death of a Democracy*. John Murray Publishers Ltd.

Karl Von Vorys (2015). *Democracy Without Consensus: Communalism and Political Stability in Malaysia*. Princeton University Press.

Kuppusamy, B. (2006, March 24). "Racism alive and well in Malaysia." *Asia Times*. Retrieved February 2015 from http://www.atimes.com/atimes/Southeast_Asia/HC24Ae01.html.

Liana Chua (2012). *The Christianity of Culture: Conversion, Ethnic Citizenship, and the Matter of Religion in Malaysian Borneo*. Palgrave Macmillan.

Lopez, G. (2010, May 22). May 13, 1969. New Mandala. Retrieved July 29, 2015, from http://asiapacific.anu.edu.au/newmandala/2010/05/22/may-13-1969/.

Mohamad, Y. D. (Director) (1991, February 27). "Malaysia: The Way Forward" (Vision 2020). The inaugural meeting of the Malaysian Business Council held on February 28,1991. Lecture by YAB Dato' Seri Dr Mahathir Mohamad, Prime Minister of Malaysia. Kuala Lumpur, Malaysia.

"New Economic Policy." The Official Website of the Economic Planning Unit, Prime Minister's Department Malaysia. 2013. Accessed July 29, 2015. http://www.epu.gov.my/en/dasar-ekonomi-barup_p_id=56_INSTANCE_Ia0Q&p_p_lifecycle=0&p_p_state=normal &p_p_mode=view&p_p_col_id=column-4&p_p_col_count=1&page=1.

"Race War in Malaysia." *Time*. 23 May 1969. Retrieved July 29, 2015.

"Report of the Federation of Malaya Constitutional Commission," 1957. London: Her Majesty's Stationary Office. Colonial No. 330. Accessed July 29, 2015. http://www.krisispraxis.com/Constitutional Commission 1957.pdf

Rezvani, S. (2015). "Five Trends Driving Workplace Diversity In 2015." Retrieved August 21, 2015.

Rothstein, R. (2014, November 12). "The Racial Achievement Gap, Segregated Schools, and Segregated Neighborhoods—A Constitutional Insult." Retrieved August 21, 2015, from http://www.epi.org/publication/the-racial-achievement-gap-segregated-schools-and-segregated-neighborhoods-a-constitutional-insult/

The House Joint Resolution proposing the 13th amendment to the Constitution, January 31, 1865; Enrolled Acts and Resolutions of Congress, 1789-1999; General Records of the United States Government; Record Group 11; National Archives

Wing, N. (2014, August 14). "When The Media Treats White Suspects And Killers Better Than Black Victims." *Huffington Post*.

Yacob, S. (2006). "Political Culture and Nation Building: Whither Bangsa Malaysia?" *Malaysian Journal of Social Policy and Society* 3, 22-42.

Part 2

Asia Leadership Fellowship

Chapter 6

The Growth of Internet Companies in China:

Adaptability and Market Awareness

Evelyn Peiqi Ooi Widjaja

Ed.M., Harvard Graduate School of Education

● ● ●

Alibaba: China's Online Marketplace

2010—My First Interaction with Alibaba

It was 2010. I was heading to China for a semester-long exchange program. Sitting on a plane from Malaysia and heading to Wuhan, a secondary city with a population at the time of 10 million people, I was unaware of the development of the e-commerce industry in China. What I got to know of the industry in my first few weeks there caught me by surprise.

Although I had gone to a primary school where classes were taught in Mandarin, my vocabulary was not strong. The terms used in China were different from those used in Malaysia or Singapore. I did not know the names of household items like screwdrivers or kitchen shelves. Thankfully, I was staying in an apartment with a fellow Singaporean, Wan Xian, who was also an exchange student and had majored in teaching Mandarin as a second language. She was about to buy a few household items on the e-commerce platform, Taobao, and asked whether I wanted to purchase some items too.

"I'll be purchasing a few laundry bags on Taobao—do you want any?" she asked.

"Um, help me buy two, please," I replied, doubting that any item purchased online would arrive on time or be similar to those in the picture.

At that time, Taobao, which is owned by Alibaba, was an e-commerce platform already popular among the Chinese. In 2010, it had 370 million users.[1] The company was founded in 1999 by Mr. Jack Ma as a business-to-business platform called Alibaba.com. In 2003, the company launched Taobao, a consumer-to-consumer platform that parallels eBay. Taobao soon gained credibility among consumers in China, despite anecdotes of companies using it to sell products of inferior quality or products that did not match the product description.

During my five-month stay in China, I noticed that Alibaba used an escrow payment system called Alipay, which holds on to the money during the transaction between the buyer and seller and only releases it to the seller once the product has been delivered. This ensures that sellers ship out products that match the product description, which increases Taobao's credibility. It is convenient to make comparisons between Alipay and PayPal, but Alipay's integrated escrow

---

1   "Taobao has 370 million users," Willis Wee, *TechinAsia*, Jan 25 2011, https://www.techinasia.com/taobao-370-million-users/. Accessed on September 6, 2015.

service catered to the market, as a deeper mistrust existed between sellers and buyers. During Taobao's early days, in 2004 to 2005, it was competing with eBay China for market share. Its flashier website appealed to customers, as compared to eBay China's site, which had a business-like interface similar to its U.S. platform. Taobao also included instant-messaging services, as Chinese users were more comfortable using their mobile phones than the internet,[2] and offered an online rating system similar to eBay's, which reduced the propensity for sellers to offer fake products. Eventually Taobao dominated the consumer-to-consumer internet retailing market share, which led to eBay's exit from China in 2006. Taobao's understanding of Chinese consumers helped the platform become a popular place for consumers to buy products online. Within a few days, a package was delivered to our doorstep. It arrived sooner than I had expected. Costing barely a dollar, my two laundry bags were of above-average quality, as promised in the product description.

Since that time, Alibaba has grown into one of China's (and the world's) biggest internet companies and has used its profits to develop two other platforms—Aliexpress and T-mall—for international and local transactions, respectively, between businesses and consumers.

2014—Using Alibaba's International Arm, Aliexpress

Alibaba's reach vastly increased since my first experience with it in 2010. In January 2014, I was preparing for my wedding. My fiancé's family was tasked with making chocolate cookies as mini-gifts for all

---

2   "How EBay failed in China," Helen H. Wang, *Forbes*, Sep 13 2010, http:// www.forbes.com/sites/china/2010/09/12/how-ebay-failed-in-china/. Accessed on September 6, 2015.

280 guests. We needed gift boxes at a low price, and after searching through our options, we decided to purchase them from Aliexpress, Alibaba's international business-to-consumer platform. Through the platform, we bought 300 gift boxes at only forty cents per box, with no shipping costs. They did, however, take a month to arrive. Alibaba's strategy of charging zero commission (or a very low rate) helped it reach a high growth rate in a very short time. In 2010, Aliexpress offered 10 million products. In 2011, the number doubled.[3]

In the past three years, the company has received an increase in returned goods in its China market, due to complaints about the authenticity of the goods. It has acted quickly to circumvent this problem by setting up quality checks, though these are not infallible. T-mall businesses are also increasingly obtaining their goods from tariff-free zones in China such as in Shanghai and Tianjin, which reduces transportation costs and ensures the authenticity of products. It is clear that Alibaba still faces considerable challenges, many of them specific to China, but it is taking active steps to maintain its credibility.

Although business analysts have tried to make comparisons between Alibaba and Amazon, Alibaba's business model differs. While Amazon charges its consumers for its services, Alibaba depends on advertisements for revenue. Far from being a Copy-to-China company, a term used for Chinese businesses that copy successful business models from foreign countries, Alibaba has adapted to market demands in China and introduced new products and innovation that are beyond

---

3   "What is Aliexpress? A history," *AliExpressChannel*, Youtube, May 7 2013, https://www.youtube.com/watch?v=tiB07OFwEO8, accessed on September 6, 2015.

Amazon's current offerings.

In this paper I will discuss the methods and innovations of three Chinese companies—Alibaba, Tencent, and, to a smaller extent, Baidu—that have grown to be the largest internet companies in China today.

Tencent—The Market-Sensitive Company

In July 2015, I traveled to Beijing with the Asia Leadership Trek to teach students how to overcome their immunity to change. It was an exciting trip for me, as I was eager to try teaching socio-emotional skills through a workshop. As with my 2010 trip to Wuhan, however, I was unprepared for the vast changes in the internet landscape in China.

We were staying in a hotel twenty minutes away from the teaching location. As I was the only ALT Fellow who could speak fluent Mandarin, I was tasked with calling two cabs for the Fellows every morning. Beijing's traffic is notorious: during peak hours cars can take double to triple the amount of time usually spent on the road. Every day, I asked the front desk to call for cabs an hour ahead of schedule to avoid traffic. The front desk used Didi Kuaidi, a Chinese Uber-style app, to book cabs for us. My strategy of being early and notifying the front desk was successful on most days, except on one day when it rained, which inadvertently increased my understanding of internet companies in China.

Two students from the workshop we conducted were sharing rooms with two of our Fellows. As they were about to leave, I asked them whether it would be possible to help us book two cabs, to which they hastily agreed. To my surprise, instead of booking cabs

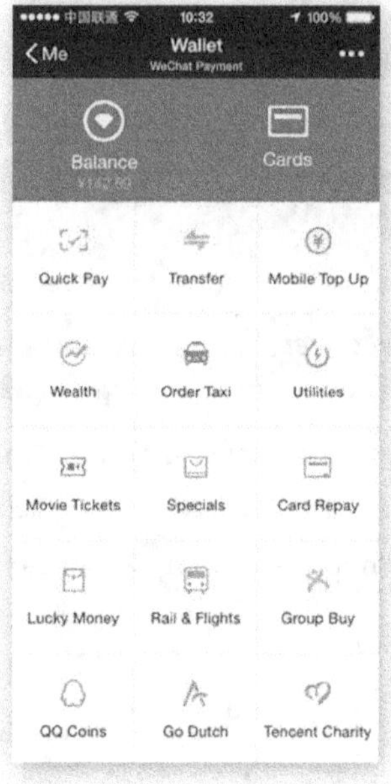

via Didi Kuaidi, they promptly opened the popular Chinese social-media app, WeChat, a subsidiary of the umbrella company Tencent. Within ten minutes, they were successful in booking a cab each. I was fascinated by this development, as Whatsapp, one of the largest social-messaging applications (reckoned by number of users) in the world, solely focuses on enhancing its communication tools, such as messaging, calling, and sending photos and videos, rather than on offering complementary products and services. Furthermore, the front desk had tried to book cabs via the Didi Kuaidi app for at least half an hour, to no avail.

As we made our way to Beihang University, I quizzed Richard, one of the students who had helped us, on the integration of a transportation app with a social-media app. "How do you book cabs via We-Chat?" I asked.

"It's fairly simple," he replied. "Although WeChat is a social-messaging app, it has other applications built into its platform. It's linked not only to Didi Kuaidi but to applications that allow users to buy movie tickets, transfer money via WeChat Payment, and other functions. After using WeChat to call for cabs, we can either use a credit card linked to WeChat Payment or use a WeChat Payment account to make payments." Richard showed me a range of applications on the platform, displayed in a three-by-five matrix.

The WeChat Payment function is unique in that it allows users either to deposit money into an account—similar to PayPal and Alipay—or link users' credit cards to the system. Both methods allow users to make payment on any item purchased via WeChat. At first glance, this function seemed like a natural development for the social-messaging application, complementing its functions. The WeChat Payment function however, is a direct competitor of Alipay, and its influence extends beyond transactions made via WeChat, as we will see in the next section.

The integration of WeChat's social-messaging function with such functions as a taxi-booking app, donating to charity, and transferring money to friends means that WeChat is one of the most frequently used applications in China. According to iResearch data, in February 2014 WeChat took close to 80 percent of share in social-media apps in China, measured by time usage.[4] This is comparable to Facebook's

---

4   "China's Top Mobile Social Apps by Time Usage," Incitez China, *China Internet Watch*, May 13 2014, http://www.chinainternetwatch.com/7481/chinas-top-mobile-social-apps-by-time-usage/, accessed on September 6, 2015.

popularity as a social-messaging app, as 73 percent of mobile-phone users age eighteen and above in the U.S. have downloaded Facebook as of July 2015.[5] WeChat offers more functions than Facebook, though Facebook has made more advancements in harnessing its data to offer users a personal experience, such as selecting stories from friends to be published on a user's "Home" page based on how frequently those stories are viewed. Since its launch in 2011, WeChat has grown to be a seamless application that pervades many areas of users' lives—traveling, online purchasing, and playing games.

WeChat's innovations are conducted in-house as well as through acquisitions of other companies. In February 2015, in line with the Lunar New Year tradition of giving out red packets of money to unmarried singles, WeChat launched Lucky Money, by which users attempt to get money from WeChat by continuously clicking on the Lucky Money link. WeChat's Lucky Money campaign was launched at a suitable time and responded to consumers' demand. Besides that, WeChat has acquired companies such as Dianping, a popular group-buying website, and integrated it into its platform. WeChat's reach is startlingly extensive. It has the potential to tap onto a large amount of personal data and tailor its offerings to its users.

As our cab pulled onto the driveway of Beihang University, I was relieved to discover that we had arrived just in time for our workshop. We stepped out of the cab, and I realized that Richard was negotiating with the cab driver. I stayed behind to assist with the negotiation. Apparently, since the cab had been booked via WeChat, WeChat Pay-

---

5   "Facebook and Google are dominating app use in the U.S.," Valentina Zarya, *Fortune*, Sep 4 2015, http://fortune.com/2015/09/04/facebook-smartphone-app/, accessed on September 6, 2015.

ment was the only way we could complete the transaction. Richard did not have enough money in his WeChat Payment account, and he did not have a credit card linked to the account. He had to either top up his account or ask his friends to transfer money to him. In a moment of panic, Richard did not use either method. Instead, he asked the cab driver to transfer money to him.

"Yes, I have transferred 100 Yuan to you," said the driver.

"Thank you, *shifu*. I will transfer 84.70 Yuan to you," Richard replied, referring to the cab fare.

I dug out 100 Yuan and handed it to the driver, completing the complicated transaction.

This incident allowed me to understand that the Chinese market is fundamentally different from that of the U.S. It is a market with a high level of trust in big internet companies, yet it struggles with creating a society that includes integrity among its core values. On the other hand, individual transactions are often completed on a person-to-person basis rather than according to a fixed set of rules, as with the transaction between the cab driver and Richard, who deemed each other to be trustworthy individuals. WeChat might have started as an imitation of foreign companies, but it has developed to become a product that caters specifically to the demands of the China market. The payment process I had witnessed was messy, but it was worth considering, for it hinted at the reasons behind the success of WeChat and China's other dominant internet companies. These companies have poised themselves strategically amidst the megatrends that have shaped China since it opened its market in the 1980s.

Societal Trends that Have Shaped China's Consumer Landscape

Trend 1: A Rising Middle Class

Never before has the world seen such a large group of people leaving poverty and entering the middle class in such a short span of time. In 2000, 4 percent of urban households in China belonged to the middle class. In 2012, that number rose to two-thirds.[6] One of the reasons behind this astronomical increase was the growing number of jobs available in the government's state-owned enterprises and in private companies that were previously not allowed to operate in the market. The new employees in these companies formed a large class of people who experienced an unexpected and large increase in their disposable income, and this new middle class was very open to spending income on new products and services like WeChat and T-mall.[7]

Trend 2: Urbanization

Besides the rapid growth of its middle class, in the last few decades China has also seen the largest migration to cities in its history. According to World Bank, China had a 19 percent urbanization rate in 1980. In 2014, that figure was 54 percent.[8] Denser social networks

---

6   "Half a Billion: China's Middle-Class Consumers," Dominic Barton, *The Diplomat*, May 30 2013. http://thediplomat.com/2013/05/half-a-billion-chinas-middle-class-consumers/. Accessed on September 20, 2015.

7   "China's E-tail Revolution," Richard Dobbs et al. *McKinsey Global Institute Report*, March 2013. http://www.mckinsey.com/insights/asia-pacific/china_e-tailing. Accessed on September 27, 2015.

8   "World Development Indicators – Urban Population (percent in total)".

are created in urban environments, which make the introduction of certain services viable. For example, Tencent partnered with a Beijing bank to offer services such as the booking of hospital appointments online. On a daily basis, China's food delivery service platform, Ele. me, receives more than 9.5 million USD in food orders in 260 cities in China.[9] Additionally, the high ownership of smartphones among the emerging middle class in cities provides a convenient platform on which companies can offer their services through applications.

Trend 3: A Consumeristic Mindset

With the opening up of markets in China, an ever-expanding range of goods and services is becoming available. Chinese citizens are spoiled for choice when it comes to shopping for goods, from clothing to electronic appliances, and, culturally, Chinese people today tend to be open to trying new products and services,[10] as long as they fit into their lifestyle. Consumers also tend to be loyal to certain products or brands once proven to be of quality.[11] This willingness to engage with the market and purchase both familiar and unknown goods and services means that new internet businesses stand a good chance of finding a foothold in the market.

World Bank, accessed on September 20, 2015.

9   "Food Delivery Service Ele.me is now China's Third-most Funded Startup," Michael De Waal-Montgomery, *VentureBeat*, August 31 2015, http://venturebeat.com/2015/08/31/food-delivery-service-ele-me-is-now-chinas-third-most-funded-startup/. Accessed on September 19, 2015.

10 "Mapping China's Middle Class," Dominic Barton, Yougang Chen and Amy Jin, *McKinsey Quarterly*, http://www.mckinsey.com/insights/consumer_and_retail/mapping_chinas_middle_class, accessed on September 20, 2015.

11 Ibid.

Factors that Have Contributed to the Rise of the Giants

Factor 1: Transforming Companies to Adapt to Market Trends

Tencent was launched in 1999. It created the internet-messaging platform QQ, which was popular in China and equivalent to MSN at that time. In 2011, it launched WeChat, which was opportune time as smartphone users increased from 143 million users in 2010 to 253 million users in 2011.[12] In 2013, it launched a voice-chat function in WeChat, allowing users to record voice messages and transmit the files to both individual and group chats. This function was popular among users and was suitable for the market, as China's telecommunications companies do not offer voice-messaging systems to users. In the ensuing years, it launched yet more functions, including mobile games and apps allowing users to purchase group-buy coupons via WeChat.

Since WeChat's introduction to the market, Tencent has shifted its focus away from QQ and toward WeChat as its key social-messaging platform. During my 2010 trip to China, the predominant parting phrase between acquaintances, indicated a desire to keep in touch, was "Do you have a QQ account?" In 2015, that phrase had changed to "What is your WeChat ID?"—a sign of changing times in China.

---

12 "Mobile Gaming in China," David Liu, Red Atoms, http://www.slideshare.net/sprie-stanford/david-liu-of-redatoms-mobile-gaming-in-china, accessed on September 6, 2015.

Factor 2: Tapping into Latent Demand

During our time in Beijing on the Trek, the Fellows went out for dinner at a pizza place with friends. Having checked that the restaurant would accept Visa or Mastercard, the Fellows went to the restaurant without worrying about whether we had enough cash in hand.

We thoroughly enjoyed ourselves. We even ordered a 32-inch pizza, the largest pizza I had ever seen—and also one of the most expensive pizzas I ever ordered, at 500 Yuan. The extravagance increased our cost significantly beyond the cash we had on hand, which was approximately 900 Yuan. The total bill added up to 1,350 Yuan.

As we parted ways with our new friends, Rachel and I went to make our payment at the counter. To our surprise, the woman at the desk told us that the restaurant did not accept Visa or Mastercard, which made us feel that they had broken their word. It accepted UnionPay, the equivalent in China, but of course this did not help us.

The waitress's subsequent question was unexpected. "Do you have WeChat? You can make payment using it."

Apparently, if one of us had had a WeChat Payment account or a UnionPay card attached to our WeChat account, we could have used it to pay for things even outside the realm of WeChat. Unfortunately, as I explained to the woman, we were foreigners and thus did not have any of the needed accounts. Feeling frustrated, Rachel and Adam went to withdraw money from a nearby ATM and eventually made the payment.

The incident, though irritating, revealed to me that WeChat has responded to the latent consumer demand to make payments during outings via its platform. Besides the pizza restaurant we went to, many other approved merchants, including 7-11 convenient stores and local pharmacies, will accept WeChat payments. As mentioned in the previous section, WeChat Payment is a direct competitor to AliPay, which launched a payment system in KFC China in July 2015. Alipay can also be used to make payment in supermarket chains such as Carrefour and Walmart.

Third-party platforms like WeChat Payment and Alipay are disrupting traditional banking methods. More people are using these platforms to make payments rather than using their credit cards. In 2011, a law was passed to regulate third-party platforms, requiring them to register themselves. This however, has not hindered the growth of these companies.

Factor 3: Closing the Gap between Businesses and Consumers

Besides being a useful platform for consumers, WeChat also caters to businesses' demands. When we were nearing the end of our workshop, I asked one of my students, Lacey, how she got to know about the workshop.

"Through WeChat," she said. She explained that businesses can open Subscription Accounts on WeChat that allow them to send one message a day to its subscribers. Typically, businesses use these accounts to market activities and to engage with their followers. "Even I could set up a Subscription Account to market my ideas or products," she said, emphasizing that it can be done free of cost.

The Subscription Account is suitable for small businesses that send out small quantities of messages. Businesses that intend to send out more messages can pay to be upgraded to a Business Account, which allows businesses to broadcast unlimited messages a day. For now,

Business Accounts are available only to businesses based in China, but this was the type of account that the partner of the Center for Asia Leadership Initiatives used to engage with its followers.

"I subscribe to their account, and through the broadcasts made, I learned of the workshop," Lacey said.

Not only can businesses use WeChat Business Accounts to broadcast advertisements, it can also create group chats to engage with its followers or potential buyers. Lacey explained that our China partner had created multiple group chats with potential participants and aired free online lectures to market the workshop. This drew in several participants, who registered for the workshop via the partner's website. The combination of messages broadcast and information shared via group chats helped the partner amass participants, who then shared information about the workshop with their friends through the Moments function, which is similar to Facebook's "update status" function. The overall effect was the creation of a network, as information shared by the business was broadcasted to other WeChat users through followers who shared the advertisement or online lecture via Moments.

Thanks to this system, the distance between businesses and users is reduced, creating a closer relationship. The development is appropriate for a high-content society like China, as it creates camaraderie between businesses and consumers and reduces misunderstanding. "To do business in China, it is a must to have a WeChat account," the CEO of the partner company said during our closing ceremony. Perhaps, thus far, this is the best way for businesses to advertise at a low cost with maximum reach.

Financial Innovations—Pushing the Limits

The revenues amassed by Alibaba and Tencent have given them sufficient cash flow to create other products. Some of these products generate more cash flow for the companies, allowing them to create and acquire other businesses. Intrigued by the possibility of further innovations, I asked one of my students, Coco, who was in Singapore in August 2015, "What new offerings do Alibaba, Tencent, and Baidu have?"

"I invest in Yuebao, which is Alibaba's mutual trust fund," she said.

I was again surprised at the development and innovation of this company. Creating Alipay seemed like a logical business decision, as it complements the company's e-commerce platforms. But this was the first time I had heard of an e-commerce company creating a mutual trust fund. "Can anyone invest in it?" I queried.

"Yes, so as long as you have a Chinese ID and a Chinese bank account," she replied. "I initially invested a small sum of money in it. I thought it was a great idea, as there is no holding period required. I can take my money in and out as I wish. When it was first launched in 2013, the rate of return was 5 percent or 6 percent, which was higher than the 3 percent-on-average yield rate for most bank accounts in China. It was a logical decision to place my money there. And, conveniently, I can also use the money to make purchases."

Such an account has at least two functions; it operates as a savings account for internet-savvy Chinese citizens and as a spending account to make purchases both online and with physical merchants. The simplicity of the idea struck me: the system benefits both the consumer and Alibaba, as Alibaba can use the money to make investments and expand the company. The risks for the consumers are larger than those of a savings account at a bank, but nevertheless Yuebao has grown in less than two years to reach 578 billion Yuan, as of June 2015.[13]

Coco explained that some time in 2014, the government imposed restrictions on Yuebao, which caused Yuebao's high yield rates to drop to about 3 percent to 4 percent, a rate similar to the government-run banks in China. Big internet companies such as Alibaba push the limits of the government by offering such services. In a country where economic growth is still largely driven by the government, it is important for private companies to toe the line. A close relationship between private companies and the government is beneficial, for the government will then give them the necessary space to grow in a government-controlled economy. Mr. Jack Ma has a close and comfortable relationship with the government. However, the rise of Yuebao shows that it is possible for private companies to stray from the government's guidelines, innovating the current systems and pushing the government to reconsider its current policies. One cannot beat the government, but at least one can test its limits.

Small and Medium-Sized Companies in China: Gobbled Up by Giants?

Besides competing with their e-payment systems, Alibaba and Tencent are acquiring and investing in similar industries that will ulti-

---

13 "Huge growth in China's money funds poses risk," Madison Marriage, June 14 2015, http://www.ft.com/intl/cms/s/0/fa4b774e-0df5-11e5-9a65-00144feabdc0.html#axzz3l1XNDZsi, accessed on September 6, 2015.

mately encroach on each other's strong suit. In 2014, Alibaba invested in ByeCity, a travel-service platform specializing in obtaining visas for Chinese nationals to travel overseas. In the same year, Tencent invested in ly.com, one of China's largest travel and booking sites. We have yet to see how these companies will compete after the investments are made, but the investments alone reveal that competition is a strong undercurrent between these two companies.

More proof of this rivalry is that in 2014 Tencent invested a 15 percent stake in JD.com, China's biggest direct-sales company and the second largest e-commerce website after Alibaba. Tencent has since integrated JD.com's functions into WeChat: users can purchase items on JD.com via WeChat and make payments via WeChat Payments. The system competes directly with Alibaba's core business.

In February 2015, Kuadi Dache and Didi Dache, which have been respectively backed by Alibaba and Tencent, merged to form Kuaidi Didi, one of the largest cab-hailing applications in the world. Baidu, on the other hand, entered into a strategic partnership with Uber in December 2014. What may seem like a mere fight between cab-hailing companies is in fact a demonstration of the strategies of these three internet giants' to gain market share in the online-to-offline market (O2O), a term commonly used in China to refer to an integration between online transactions and the physical world.

These three companies do not just compete with each other but are also seen as competing with smaller companies. Baidu bought a majority stake in a food-delivery service, Nuomi (which translates to "glutinous rice"), in 2013. The service was in direct competition with a start-up founded by Shanghai Jiaotong University students in 2009, Ele.me (which translates to "Hungry?"). In 2015, Tencent invested in Ele.me and Baidu increased its investments in Nuomi. Alibaba, on the other hand, invested in a group-buying site, Meituan, which offers food-delivery services.

One of the students I talked to said that these internet giants often wait for the smaller companies to "fight it out" before they invest in successful ones. With this in mind, some smaller companies form with the aim of selling to the giants as their ultimate goal.

By increasing their portfolio, Alibaba, Tencent, and Baidu are increasing their element of stickiness—the likelihood that users will continue to use the services they offer. Their stickiness also ensures that users will be less likely to move to other platforms, as they trust the applications and have integrated them into their lifestyles.

In China, Alibaba, Tencent, and Baidu have become synonymous with e-commerce, social messaging, and internet searching respectively. In many ways they are dramatically different from their seeming equivalents in the U.S., having tailored their offerings to the Chinese market and to Chinese cultural expectations. Each company, however, is investing steadily in companies that support both its core strengths and its peripheral activities, and this is one of the major similarities between the internet giants of China and the U.S.

Conclusion

China has been and still is known for being a country that copies innovations from other countries. However, the ways in which Baidu, Alibaba, and Tencent (together known as BAT) have developed show that they, at least, are not Copy-to-China companies. These companies understand the market demands of the society they operate in—

a society comprising many fast-paced cities with citizens who barely have time to have a meal, who are jaded and yet crave more consumption. They also understand the trends defining 21st century in China: a rising middle class, a consumeristic mindset, and urbanization. By tapping onto their knowledge of the market and their understanding of the trends that will affect China's future, these companies have positioned themselves as the most forward-thinking internet companies in the country.

In the future, we will probably see more developments in the online and O2O realm from these companies, either through in-house innovation or through acquisition. This may hinder the development of small and medium enterprises, as BAT has a strong cash flow to support their innovations. Nonetheless, niche companies still exist and thrive in the world's largest domestic market. Applications such as BeautyPlus—a beautification app, popular among young girls, that makes people in photos look slimmer or fairer—have done well in China without being swallowed by BAT. In the first eight months after its launch, BeautyPlus's video-editing app, MeiPai, attracted one hundred million users in China.[14] Similarly, Chunyu Yisheng, a successful health application that allows users to consult physicians to diagnose ailments, has so far been untouched by the three big internet companies. Despite these companies' current independence, however, I suspect that once BAT sees the alignment of these companies with their businesses—or if competition begins between them and BAT

---

14 "Meet Meipai, the Chinese app with 100M users that a Facebook exec calls 'Instagram for video,'" Chris O' Brien, June 23 2015, http://venturebeat. com/2015/06/23/meet-meipai-the-chinese-app-with-100m-users-that-a-facebook-exec-calls-instagram-for-video/, accessed on September 6, 2015.

companies in these areas—we will see these smaller niche companies being bought or invested in by the three giants.

Although BAT has seen much success in China, it is still subjected to government regulations, as seen in the case of Yuebao of Alibaba. Building a strong relationship with the government remains an important task, as the government still has the power to shut down private companies if they interfere with government plans and values. Alibaba could have easily suffered the closure of Yuebao, had it not been for Mr. Ma's close relationship with the government. It is thus in the interest of all companies that operate in China to build a close relationship with government officials, in order to ensure the continuance and development of their businesses.

Powerful though BAT has become, the three companies still have room for improvement. One area that BAT could focus on in the future is harnessing the personal data they acquire. To some degree they have already begun: Baidu has used its data both to recommend personalized advertisements to users and to develop programs to monitor diseases, offer a Lunar New Year travel visualization map, and predict flu outbreaks. Alibaba has used software to map the social relationships among its users, in order to determine the foremost influencers in its networks; it also uses data to recommend personalized products to users. Tencent is lagging behind in exploiting the potential of big data,[15] but with the push from the government to develop the big-data industry, we will almost certainly see Tencent as well as Baidu

---

15 "How Baidu, Tencent and Alibaba are leading the way in China's big data revolution," Ana Swanson, 25 Aug 2015, http://www.scmp.com/tech/innovation/article/1852141/how-baidu-tencent-and-alibaba-are-leading-way-chinas-big-data, accessed on September 6, 2015.

and Alibaba delving into their data in the near future.

The Asia Leadership Trek taught me never to underestimate the capability of Chinese companies. Walking on the streets of Zhongguanchun—China's equivalent of the Silicon Valley—on the last day of the Trek, I sensed that I was at the crux of innovation in Beijing. We were heading to ALT's partner's headquarters, and I saw Microsoft on my right and Baidu nearby. Chinese companies such as these have strong potential, despite not receiving much content coverage in the English-speaking world. In the West there is still a strong perception that Chinese goods and services are of inferior quality, and Western media's disapproval of China's one-party political system exacerbates the West's suspicion of Chinese businesses. Within China, there seems to be a lack of understanding that cooperation between the BAT companies and the government would bring about positive social change and economic development in China—change that would be enormously beneficial to the country's citizens. Nevertheless, although my students often grouse about the authoritarian rule of the government, they also recognize that the speedy economic development of the last thirty years is partly attributable to government-led policies.

My experience on the Trek confirmed my vision of an innovative and adaptable online economic scene in China; what I saw there deepened my interest in the internet companies' development and promise, and I have enjoyed researching the topic in both English and Mandarin, deepening my own understanding of the topic, and sharing my knowledge in order to increase Western understanding of Chinese businesses.

Acknowledgments

I would like to acknowledge the help of Lacey Liu, Richard Zhu, Coco Zhang, and Steven Zeng, whose insights gave me a greater understanding of the development of internet companies in China.

| Chapter 7 |

Perceptions of Creativity in Asia:

Leading the Trek's Workshops in Design Thinking

Jaye Buchbinder

MSE, Stanford University

●●●

Introduction

Before the 2015 Asia Leadership Trek began this summer, I found it difficult to know how my workshops in design thinking would be received. On the one hand, the Chinese start-up economy is booming and the Japanese attention to detail in design is renowned. I had also become friends with the design-thinking Fellow from the previous Trek, a person widely regarded as a favorite among students. On the other hand, I recognized that, coming from Stanford Engineering, where "design thinking" belongs with "the cloud" and "big data" as a major buzz word, I was in an isolated bubble. In fact, I wasn't entirely sure if people outside my small Palo Alto community knew much at all about design thinking, even in the United States.

Design thinking is essentially a toolkit of frameworks and approaches, combined with an adaptable mindset that helps in problem-solving. It is not, as many assume, a method for drawing aesthetically pleasing logos or making beautiful products, although it might aid in either of these tasks. Rather, design thinking centers around understanding the user and figuring out user needs in order to create an optimal solution. The moment you walk into the Stanford Design School, a humble and relatively unmarked building on the outside, the institution's zany mindset is palpable. From the walls covered in post-its to the up-beat music and the chairs scattered everywhere, it is evident that the Design School is not your average learning environment.

When I first took a design-thinking course, I did not believe in the rituals that make the crazy band of engineers in this small building seem like cult leaders. I refused to participate in the dances that opened our classes or the improv games aiming to help us connect with team members. It took two intensive weeks of experiencing the design-thinking process to find that the results of this process, with all its startling rituals, were both more creative and more effective than I had imagined. I saw improvement even in myself, in my willingness to test solutions in the real world, to challenge myself for more creative options, and to engage in a strong team rapport.

These were among the things I wanted to instill in my students on the Trek. I wanted to show them the skeleton of the design-thinking process, the essential tools for each step, and the mindset needed to solve problems creatively. I also planned to give them a taste of the wackier techniques in use at the Design School, in the hope that they would then be able to replicate those techniques after the workshop without pushing too far past their comfort zones. I expected some trepidation, but although the Trek leaders warned us about major cultural discrepancies, I did not anticipate much of what I ended up experiencing on the Trek itself.

Overall, I believe that many of the principles and techniques I discussed came across strongly, and many of the students showed both an increased understanding of design thinking and a greater appreciation of their own creative abilities. In the classes I taught and the conversations I had with individual students, I discovered a series of interesting differences between the Asian and American cultures, especially in the definition of creativity and the perceptions of personal creative ability, and also a surprising array of similarities, particularly in the conflict of "fluffy" versus "tech" and the importance of empathy building. Ultimately, what struck me most vividly on the Trek was the benefit of international cooperation.

The Definition of Creativity

Creativity, in my definition, means solving a problem in a more innovative and effective way than previous solutions. In a 2014 *Fast Company* article on Silicon Valley creativity, Mr. Soren Kaplan talks about using a diverse group of talent, working with users, and scaling to support innovation (Kaplan, 2014). The only similarity that I found between these elements and the culture for creativity in China was the importance placed on the ability to scale. With the country's population quickly approaching one and a half billion people, the need to utilize and respond to China's broad demographic is obvious. Winning the market in China means both a huge revenue and an enormous growth potential.

Major differences between Chinese and American innovation became quickly apparent on the 2015 Summer Trek, even before our first workshop began. While touring the Forbidden Palace, we saw ornate emperor's quarters, gold-leaf designs, and massive gardens for the royal family. I was blown away by the designs, and as a native of Southern California, a place with a relatively short history, I was impressed by the levels of history on display in the middle of a major city. Alongside these beautiful buildings, I also noticed the ubiquity of international fashion brands: shirts that screamed "CHLOEE," "VERSACHEY," and other almost correctly spelled designer names covered the streets of Beijing.

Forbes recently published an exposé of stores in China that look almost identical to Apple stores, even down to the products they sell, but are not, in fact, Apple stores (Forbes, 2015). Similarly, we saw cars that closely resembled Range Rovers, only to discover that they were imitation cars. The trend of imitation sheds some light on the entrepreneurial spirit in China. The general concept is to take a product that already works and duplicate it in order to gain control of a portion of that particular market sector. Although the practice would not be legal under trademark practices in the United States, many successful Chinese companies are based off of ideas from elsewhere and adapted to the Chinese culture. For instance, in a *Business Insider* article, Chinese Entrepreneur Mr. Bowei Gai writes that there are "5,000 Groupon clones, and over 100 Android stores" (Rosoff, 2011).

One reason for the cloning trend is that many international companies, including Facebook and Google, are not allowed to operate in China. As a result, Chinese companies jump at the opportunity to fill the void. Unlike the start-up culture in the Silicon Valley, where new ideas show up every day, Chinese investors expect previously tested ideas before they risk investment. Often successful clones, such as Baidu or WeChat, differ substantially from their base companies, as they have been altered to fit the Chinese market, but the original DNA of the concepts remain. It is difficult to see the creativity in this system when you come from a culture where copying is not heralded as innovative, but the rise of Beijing's own Silicon Valley proves that it can be a successful route, especially when the base companies are not allowed within the borders.

Replication was also a dominant theme among the students we worked with. Classrooms in Asia are a far cry from the circus environment I had experienced at the Design School, which weaves together a blend of lecture, activity, and demonstration. On the Trek, nearly all the students we spoke with told us they were used to being lectured to and then taking notes and memorizing. In Malaysia, one of the students' major concerns was the difficulty of memorizing the vast quantity of information necessary to pass their final exams. While many of my engineering exams were open-book and open-note in order to avoid this issue of over-memorizing, students in Malaysia are taught to memorize the teachers' lectures verbatim and then replicate them on the tests. The system yields strong study skills and discipline, but also a near-total lack of creativity.

This lack was most apparent during the brainstorming exercise I ran in the last design-thinking workshop for each conference, in which students brainstormed ways to retain and disseminate the knowledge they had learned in the previous four days. Without fail, taking notes and reviewing the notes were the first proposed ideas.

At least three times, a group misunderstood the prompt as a question of what they had learned. These groups immediately referred to their notes, wrote down everything that had been discussed in the previous days, and posted them on the walls as ideas. While part of this miscommunication stemmed from the language barrier, another aspect of it came from the instinct, instilled in Malaysian schools, to write down all of the information already received.

This cultural difference brings us to the another element of creativity, hinging on the difference between cooperation and development. In a Stanford course I took with Ms. Heidi Roizen, "The Spirit of Entrepreneurship," she explained that companies with multiple founders, especially founders who have worked together before, are more likely to get funding. In our Design School classes, we are taught that one plus one equals more than two: collaboration yields larger results than solo brainstorming.

In the Asian countries we visited on the Trek, however, the students tended to work alone rather than in groups, with the exception of some of the young professionals. In my workshop's first brainstorming exercise, the students tended to come up with ideas individually rather than using the energy of their teams. Mr. Martin Attiq, a fellow Trekker, suggested that I include a demonstration of working in a group before introducing the brainstorming exercise, precisely because the idea of working with others is unfamiliar to students educated in a memorization-based system.

In design thinking, an important element is the concept of idea recognition. Everyone tends to look for proof that they are the strongest member of the group, no matter their upbringing or native country. It is ingrained in the human psyche to seek this social proof, and when it comes to ideas, the desire to excel translates into an urge either to keep your own idea separate, if you think it is the best, or to avoid contribution, if you fear a judgment on its quality. We saw the first of these trends exhibited when we visited the start-up Career Dream in Beijing, a successful company that offers workshops and training sessions to help place students in jobs in the finance and consulting sectors. The head of the company was an ambitious and driven man, who had a lot to say about where he had come from and about his pride in the company. It was interesting to listen to a founder speak with some arrogance about his personal story and take full credit for his firm. Although similar feats aren't unheard of in the United States, it was striking that this major firm is a solo venture. The founder's confidence and bravado undoubtedly help him survive in the competitive and fast-paced Chinese market, where companies are easily squelched by regulation.

Overall, it seemed that the Asian definition of creativity focused more on making companies successful in a new environment rather than on innovation in ideas, the definition that fuels creative ventures in America's Silicon Valley. However, my colleagues at Stanford have pointed out two caveats that I should address in these observations. The first is that Stanford and the Silicon Valley, while famous for their innovative culture, are not microcosms of American culture; rather, they represent only a small segment of the population, one that embraces an intense study of innovation. The second is that the students we met in Asia on the Trek were usually younger than university age, we interacted with only a small number of them, and even fewer of those were specifically studying innovation. This means that our window into the nature of creativity in Asia was necessarily quite limited.

Is Creativity a Bone or a Muscle?

One overlap between Asian and American students is their definition of personal creativity. Among my American friends and colleagues alike, with the possible exception of my peers in the mechanical-engineering product-design program at Stanford, most people do not consider themselves creative. This is also true in Asia, but even more so, as the students believe that creativity is an intrinsic rather than a built trait. At the beginning of my workshops, I asked the students to raise their hands if they thought they were creative. Only in Malaysia, at the Asia Leadership Youth (ALY) Camp, did more than one student raise a hand, and even then it was only two.

Many of the students I worked with defined creativity as the ability to draw well, envision aesthetic objects, or come up with wild ideas; they suggested that these abilities are tied to a fixed portion of your brain. To counteract this belief, I told them that creativity is a muscle that can be developed rather than a bone that stays the same into adulthood. I also introduced them to an article by Mr. David Kelley and his brother in the *Harvard Business Review*, entitled "Reclaim Your Creative Confidence." Essentially, the Kelleys suggest that the practice of empathy and of pushing past your comfort zone into new projects and challenges helps develop the creative muscle (Kelley and Kelley, 2012). I reaffirmed this notion with a video of Mr. David Kelley explaining his ideas and then told the story of my own journey into creativity.

I did not consider myself a creative person before taking design-thinking courses at Stanford. Coming in, I anticipated studying neuroscience in a pre-medicine track, with the aim of eventually going to medical school and becoming a neurosurgeon. But after spending freshman year in the pre-med track and feeling completely burnt out on chemistry, I took an environmental engineering course and fell in love. Still, it wasn't until my junior year, when I stumbled into the Design School, that I learned the process of understanding users and thus began to understand the technical side of creativity.

Creativity is a useful skill regardless of your profession. The creativity I have developed through the Design School plays a large part in my ability to excel in other parts of my life, especially in my engineering courses. In my course on chemical engineering, we had to use our knowledge of battery capacity and renewable energy to create a system that could supply the entire country with energy. Like the other students, I focused on one type of energy and on the book we had been supplied with, but it was my design-school knowledge—the idea that creating a solution requires understanding the problem—that pushed me to look outside the boundaries. I spoke to experts in the fields of battery design and electric vehicles as well as regular citizens in order to craft an innovative solution.

Creativity not only aids design and engineering processes, it also makes them more fun and meaningful. By striving to understanding the user, you can develop a deeper connection to the problem you are solving, and the more original your solution is, the more driven you are to make it succeed. This became apparent to my students during our exercises in problem-solving analysis, which my colleague Mr. Attiq and I ran almost every week. At the beginning of a three-hour session, we presented the students with a problem and walked them through the process of acquainting themselves with both the problem itself and the stake-holding groups. The solutions that the students came up with invariably impressed both us and their peers. My favorite solution was a response to the question of how might we retain and share the knowledge we'd gained in the past week: a group from the Asia Leadership Youth (ALY) Camp suggested getting a tattoo of what they had learned. They argued that the tattoo would not only be a daily reminder of the workshop's lessons but also stimulate discussion among their peers, creating new conversations that would advance their learning. My colleagues and I were very impressed by this insightful and out-of-the-box, if not entirely feasible, solution. None of these students had considered themselves creative at the beginning of the week.

It was frustrating to see the ubiquitous lack of creative confidence across student groups in Asia, but it was deeply rewarding to see their rapid development over the brief span of a week or less. The quick turnaround reinforced the importance and pay-off of practicing creativity and strengthened my desire to work on my own creative confidence. To me the lack of creativity ties into a larger cultural theme that was evident in all the Asian countries we visited, a theme visible even in the most creative pockets of the United States: the battle between artist and scientist.

"Fluffy" vs. "Techy"

At Stanford, there is a divide between "techy" students and "fluffy" students—students studying engineering, sciences, and math and students in the humanities programs. The major differences lie in the title of B.S. versus B.A. and the amount of time spent completing problem sets versus writing essays, but too often there is also a perceived difference in worth. The divide is exacerbated by the premium placed on engineers in the area's countless start-ups. *The New Yorker* discussed the effect of this emphasis on the university itself and received some backlash from the student community as a result (Auletta, 2012). The issue often provokes controversy, but the fundamental divide at Stanford between the value placed on the arts and the value placed on the sciences is undeniable.

I was surprised when we came across a similar issue in the Asian student groups we visited. One major theme that came up for the first time in Beijing and became more and more prominent as we traveled was the eagerness students felt—an eagerness accompanied by stress and anxiety—to get into a science program. In many Asian countries, standardized testing determines whether or not you can get into a science program. The students who do not score high enough are placed into arts programs, which include subjects such as history and writing. This stratification of subjects encourages the brighter and more renowned teachers to prefer science, leaving the arts students with teachers and peers who cannot help but feel inferior to the scientists. The students in Malaysia explained to me that arts students feel less intelligent and thus less motivated than their science peers, even though their placement was the result not of their own preferences but of a single standardized test.

One Malaysian student gave a speech on her choice to follow the arts path even though she had been accepted into the science track. She told us how emotional her decision had been and how difficult it was to pursue her passion rather than bow to societal and familial pressure to follow the more prestigious path. Her parents as well as her teachers urged her to change her mind, arguing that the science track would lead to a higher-paying, more stable job. Other students echoed her sentiments, often reaching the verge of tears as they described the pressure they felt to excel in mathematics and science and the narrow strictures forcing them into certain occupations. Some of the students, of course, were passionately committed to the sciences and wanted nothing more than to pursue them. Others, however, were not so sure: one student explained that he wanted to pursue design but felt it would be a dishonor to his family. One young woman told me that she loved my course in design thinking but would never be able to call it "design thinking" when speaking to her parents; rather she would need to call it "engineering problem-solving" to justify her decision to take the workshop in the first place.

Across Asia we found students set on careers in the financial and consulting sectors, citing job security and high salaries. They were doubtful of the benefits of the unconventional mindsets of design thinking, until we proved to them the importance of problem-solving across the board. It was not an easy task. Especially with the young professionals, it was difficult to convince the workshop's participants that design thinking, creativity, and innovation would help them further their careers regardless of their field.

We spent time emphasizing the benefits of diversity of thought—the theory that communicating only with people similar to you limits your range of solutions. We explained the "similarity heuristic," the idea that people tend to make decisions based on things they already know or that are similar to the decisions of people like them. While this tendency probably evolved as a survival trait, it can be dangerous to surround yourself with like-minded people because they will only affirm what you already believe, without challenging your assumptions. To counteract this tendency, we suggested building a diverse team with a wide range of backgrounds, in order to develop a well-rounded perspective. This interdisciplinary approach becomes especially useful during brainstorming: rather than having every team member replicating each other's ideas, a diverse group often leads to unprecedented synthesis and yields results outside the normal solution set.

Deferring Judgment

In my design-thinking workshops, I tried to instill the belief in my students that when it comes to generating ideas, one plus one can equal more than two, thanks to the inspiration you can receive from your teammates. It is crucial not only to support each other but to feed off each other's energy in order to create a productive problem-solving environment. One of the brainstorming rules that reaffirms this claim is deferring judgment. The idea has two parts: deferring self-judgment and deferring judgment of the ideas of others.

The latter is fairly straightforward: do not tell your peers that you think their ideas are dumb. It shuts them down creatively, shuts down the group's energy, and stops those group-members from contributing in the future. Crucially, the method also holds true in the opposite way: you should not indiscriminately praise another's idea as soon as it is proposed. Endorsing one idea too soon can prevent others from being suggested, and thus, while positive energy is crucial, universally directing the positive energy is even more important.

Deferring self-judgment and developing self-awareness can be far more difficult. Deferring judgment on your own ideas entails blurting them out before you have evaluated them for quality. We tend to believe that our spur-of-the-moment ideas will be viewed as dumb or bad, and so we wait for a better idea to pop up, but in fact voicing those initial ideas often helps push the group past obvious first thoughts. Moreover, your ideas might spark inspiration in someone else, who might take the kernel of your suggestion and develop it in a different and more productive direction.

In Asia, I found it harder than I had anticipated to explain this concept. Every brainstorm began in near-silence because none of the group-members wanted to be the first to contribute. Sometimes one enterprising student would take over, but still the other group-members would fall back and hesitate to contribute. At other times, the group-members would separate and slowly write down ideas on their own, without verbalizing their thoughts.

After witnessing this trend in the first week, I decided to try an activity that I had encountered in Ms. Tina Seelig's course "Creativity and Innovation" during my undergraduate years at Stanford. The first step was breaking into groups and spending twenty minutes or so brainstorming things that would make a restaurant horrible. These brainstorms typically started off with "bad food" or "bad service" and then escalated to more specific ideas. The possible flaws sent the students into hysterics, ranging from "no wifi" to "serves leftover food" or "humans as food."

At this point the students had built up a substantial amount of positive energy and were starting to become more comfortable with the process. I directed each group to choose their worst idea and pass it to the group next to them. Then I introduced a shift: I announced that these terrible ideas were actually brilliant and that each group had to take the bad idea they'd been given and transform it into the basis for an award-winning restaurant. They had twenty minutes to figure out why the idea would make a restaurant compelling and why it would win an award.

Initially the students were completely spooked by this change of pace; many times they could not initially understand the prompt. But with a little encouragement they threw themselves into problem-solving, and soon they reached a high point of creative energy. The final concepts were astounding. The restaurant that served leftovers turned into an affordable option for Michelin food, while the restaurant serving humans as food endowed its patrons with the traits of their meals, so that people dining off Olympians could become world-class athletes themselves. The restaurant with no wifi became a place for family bonding, without cell interruption. Time and time again, the students were ecstatic and I was floored by their results. They began to understand that terrible ideas, reframed, can actually be brilliant, and they grasped the importance of watching ideas develop rather than judging them immediately.

The other thrilling aspect of the exercise was watching the students' creative confidence grow over less than an hour. By the end of the session, students who had initially been shy and quiet were bragging about the benefits of eating the "Michael Phelps" dish at their restaurant. Each student's creative confidence helped to strengthen the confidence of their group and their group's conviction in the development of their ideas. The group rapport that built up during this exercise helped strangers to unite in the name of collaboration and creative problem-solving. In fact, the group rapport that arose among all the attendees of the programs on the Trek was one of the most in-spirational, rewarding, and surprising aspects of our trip.

Empathy Building

In all the workshops we held, the most beneficial part of the design-thinking process was the building of empathy—getting to know your user and your problem on the deepest possible level. In the workshops we held in Malaysia and Guangzhou, we began with trips to the nearest mall, where the students interviewed passers-by on a variety of topics, from their use of umbrellas to locating stores. By the end of each workshop we had moved to political, economic, and social issues that were increasingly relevant in their lives. In our final workshop, in Japan at the Trilateral Leadership Summit, this last segment of the process took on an unprecedented importance.

We arrived in Japan with a great deal of anticipation. We had just finished two fast-paced workshops in Guangzhou and flown over-night to Sendai. At dinner that first evening, at a traditional Japanese restaurant, we spoke with the Summit organizers about the issues we were trying to tackle. Relations between Japan, Korea, and China are embittered for several reasons, including an inability to construct a consistent historical narrative across textbooks in these countries, major geographical arguments over islands, and a variety of economic and political disagreements. We would be teaching students from all three countries at the Summit, and Mr. Attiq and I would be hosting three-hour workshops on each of the four days, leading these students through the process of understanding these issues and concluding with a presentation on problem-solving.

The first day started off with minor grumbling, as we explained that the students would be interviewing their peers for an hour on the issues at hand. They began to talk to each other and soon discovered, as they later revealed in the debrief, that they had differing perspectives on the topics they covered, even within the same nationalities. Over the next four days, they spent countless hours in and out of the workshop developing their understanding of each other and crafting solutions to the problems they were discussing. When the final day came and they presented their solutions, they had developed not only pride for their ideas but also an intense, cross-cultural understanding, thanks to the international groups. Their solutions were thoughtful and creative, and they included cultural values from all three countries, as well as individual strengths from the group members. Mr. Attiq and I were extraordinarily impressed, and the students told us that they too were impressed by how much they had learned. They explained that while they had enjoyed brainstorming and the improvisational games, they had also learned a lot from these activities. The process demonstrated the importance of leaving one's own comfort zone and of approaching issues with an open, unbiased perspective. The students formed lasting bonds with people whom they had been taught to regard with suspicion. They made friendships with political enemies and formed teams across borders that are not easily crossed.

After the workshop, one of my students asked me if leaders in the United States conducted empathy interviews. I responded that I was not sure but that I knew design thinking did not typically inform the policies of many worldwide political leaders. He explained that he wanted to become a diplomat and use design thinking to understand the problems of the world. He said that empathy had aided him in getting over his fear of the students from other countries and that he thought it would be beneficial for leaders to understand their neighbors, in order to craft mutually aiding policies.

I left Japan glowing at this reaffirmation of the benefits of empathy. I knew that I was leaving groups of well-informed and inspired students who would promote creativity and design thinking in their own lives. The results of the Trek far exceeded my expectations. The students I met have the drive and conviction needed to change their communities, and the fire in their eyes has pushed me to find the change I want to make as well.

Works Cited

Auletta, Ken. April 30, 2012. "Get Rich U." *The New Yorker*. http://www.newyorker.com/magazine/2012/04/30/get-rich-u. Accessed August 20, 2015.

"China Population." Google. https://www.google.com/webhp?sourceid=chrome-instant&ion=1&espv=2&ie=UTF-8#q=china percent20population. Accessed August 20, 2015.

Photo: Fake Apple Store. *Forbes*. http://www.forbes.com/pictures/gdfd45fdkd/apple-from-the-outside-2/. Accessed August 20, 2015.

Kaplan, Soren. February 11, 2014. "Tap Into the 7 Secrets of Silicon Valley's Innovation Culture." *Fast Company*. http://www.fastcodesign.com/3026220/tap-into-the-7-secretsof-silicon-valleys-innovation-culture. Accessed August 20, 2015.

Kelley, David. March 2012. "How to Build Your Creative Confidence." TED. http://www.ted.com/talks/david_kelley_how_to_build_your_creative_confidence?language=en. August 20, 2015.

Kelley, Tom and David Kelley. December 2012. "Reclaim Your Creative Confidence." *Harvard Business Review*. https://hbr.org/2012/12/reclaim-your-creative-confidence. Accessed August 20, 2015.

Rosoff, Matt. October 31, 2011. "These Facts About the Chinese Startup Scene Will Blow Your Mind." *Business Insider Tech*. http://www.businessinsider.com/when-it-comes-to-startups-in-china-everything-you-think-you-know-is-wrong-2011-10. Accessed August 20, 2015.

| Chapter 8 |

Teaching Negotiations in South Korea:

Insights from the Field

Eugene B. Kogan

Teaching Scholar, Harvard Kennedy School of Government

● ● ●

9/11 and Nuclear Negotiations

The smoke plume rose high above the city, starting from the ninety-second floor of the World Trade Center. It soon grew and overtook the sky, rushing through the gaps between skyscrapers. Though a safe distance from Ground Zero that morning, I witnessed the angst of a city under attack. I heard the sirens fade in and out throughout the day as first responders from across the city worked to find survivors, heal the wounded, and quench flames. Grand Central Station was shut down, and I was able to leave the city only late in the evening. The train conductor did not even collect the tickets. As passengers shared stories with one another about where they had been during the attacks, I asked myself, "What if a similar terrorist attack occurred that involved the use of nuclear weapons?"

As a child growing up in Moscow during the Cold War, I did not know what mutual assured destruction was, but I felt it. Thousands of atomic warheads pointed at major Soviet cities, and this knowledge was a deeply frightening reality. While we no longer teach children how to respond in case of a nuclear attack, nuclear weapons remain a danger: the threat of one coming under the control of a terrorist organization is as constant as the warheads of my childhood. And when 9/11 happened, I wondered, "Can we negotiate with terrorists?"

After that day, I immersed myself in the study of nuclear nonproliferation, seeking to understand how to limit the spread of nuclear weapons around the world. This work culminated in a doctoral dissertation on the subject of nuclear negotiations between the United States and its allies during the 1970s and 1980s. My research sought to understand the conditions under which the U.S.-led nuclear negotiations with allies succeeded and failed. Specifically, why did Taiwan and South Korea give up their nuclear pursuits under U.S. duress during the Cold War, while Israel and Pakistan proceeded to attain nuclear capability?

My research suggests that military or economic sanctions alone, or threats to withdraw military protection, have historically been less effective on their own than when they were employed in conjunction with measures aimed at derailing the technological progress of the target's nuclear-weapons program. Such measures, which I call "technology restrictions," included multilateral export controls, unilateral pressure on suppliers to abandon nuclear-technology transfers, and expert visits to the target country to dissuade scientists and political officials from pursuing the nuclear program. In short, leverage matters in these negotiations—and in others.

Now a fellow at Harvard Kennedy School's Belfer Center for Science and International Affairs, I am working on a book that will recommend ways to prevent states from unnecessarily becoming nuclear powers. I was attracted to the Asia Leadership Trek because I love to teach and because I believe that one of the best ways to make the world safer is to teach young people and future leaders how to negotiate skillfully and effectively.

Through the Lens

I had written about North Korea, but I had never seen it before this Trek. As I stared through the large, stationary, 25-cents-per-view tourist binoculars at a North Korean soldier at a DMZ checkpoint, he briefly stared back at me. It was a chilling moment.

For young people growing up in South Korea today, the prospect of regional conflict and war is ever-present. South Korea is located at the fulcrum of international crises in East Asia. It borders a nuclear-armed and belligerent North Korea, an increasingly assertive China, and a Japan that is re-assessing its global role. With hostilities running high, complex political and economic decisions become even more challenging.

The South Korean high school students I was about to instruct in negotiations might become statesman, diplomats, civic and corporate leaders, and they would undoubtedly experience many moments like the one I had just experienced. Future South Korean diplomats will have to talk, listen, and ultimately negotiate with North Koreans. They will need to understand coercive bargaining.

The First Day

It was the first day of Harvard Week in South Korea, and high school students were filing into our small classroom. "What career path do you want to choose?" I asked.

"I want to become a CEO," said one young man.

"I want to become a diplomat," a young woman chimed in. They themselves might have been shy, taught by the Korean educational system not to challenge authority, but their dreams were bold.

Their answers made me realize that these teenagers were the people who would soon be confronting, directly or indirectly, the consequences of North Korea's regional and international behavior.

Hamburgers v. Spaghetti

The first negotiation exercise I designed required students to negotiate the choice of a meal: hamburgers or spaghetti. The exercise introduced the students to the process of reconciling conflicting interests. On the face of it, the situation had no simple solution: spaghetti and hamburgers are highly dissimilar, making agreement unlikely.

Initially, they found themselves stalemated between the hamburger and spaghetti positions. I tried explaining that to reach a mutually beneficial agreement, they had to listen for fundamental "interests" (the values that genuinely motivate the speaker) as opposed to the "positions" (the first things that the person articulates). They began digging around for interests, but they still had trouble making progress until I finally prodded them to ask the most powerful question in negotiation—why?

Once a student on one side mentioned that he wanted to eat hamburgers because they were cheap, a student on the other side quickly responded, "Spaghetti is on sale this week." These kids had never heard of "positions" or "interests," but they intuitively grasped what negotiation and compromise was all about. Ultimately, they decided on a meal of "hamburgetti"—spaghetti mixed with strips of hamburger meat. Their final compromise of "hamburgetti" was catchy and emblematic of the creative thinking these future leaders will have to employ to solve the hardest negotiation problems—like negotiating with North Korea to give up its nuclear program and to reunify the two Koreas.

Breaking Down Negotiations

Nuclear negotiations are an example of coercive bargaining, which departs in significant ways from the interests-based, deal-making framework pioneered by Harvard Law School Professor Roger Fisher and his colleagues in their famous book *Getting to Yes*. As negotiations expert Jeswald Selacuse reminds us with the title of his most recent book—*Negotiating Life*—we negotiate every day. While unschooled in negotiation concepts, the young people in South Korea often referred to negotiation issues in their lives. "What if my life and career aspirations are different from the dreams my parents have for me?" they asked.

The study of negotiation promotes critical thinking about the problems we face. From negotiation with our relatives about our professional and personal goals to bargaining with nuclear-armed adversaries, negotiation is a critical skill that we deploys almost daily.

The movie *13 Days*, about the Cuban Missile Crisis, shows that brainstorming—the skill that negotiators are encouraged to develop—paved the way for Robert McNamara to propose the idea of quarantine, which helped force Soviet leader Nikita Khrushchev to back down in 1962. In *Beyond Winning: Negotiating to Create Value in Deals and Disputes,* Professor Robert Mnookin and his colleagues explain the importance of brainstorming: "The most effective brainstorming requires real freedom—however momentary—from practical constraints." "The goal," they continue, "is to liberate those at the table to suggest ideas. … Indeed, those at the table should feel free to suggest ideas that are not in their best interest, purely to stimulate discussion, without fear that others at the table will later take those ideas as offers."

Negotiation also enables the parties involved the disagreement to increase mutual gains. By thinking outside the box about how they can work together, the parties can learn how to collaborate instead of being stalemated in their own respective positions. *Getting to Yes* is well-known for the story of the two sisters who argue over one orange. Having gotten one half of the orange, the first daughter eats the inside and throws out the peel, while the other jettisons the fruit and uses the peel as an ingredient for a cake. Had the two sisters talked about why they wanted the orange in the first place, they would have realized that their interests did not compete but, in fact, complemented each other's. One of them could have gotten to eat the whole fruit, while the other would have had more peel for the cake.

Such an agreement would only be possible, of course, if the sisters sought out each other's reasons for wanting the orange. Negotiation requires the fundamental skill of active listening—digging for the fundamental interests (e.g. baking a cake) that lie behind the stated positions (e.g. I want the orange). It is a skill crucial in both interpersonal communication and relationship-building.

Coercive Bargaining—What It Is and Why It Matters

So what about coercive negotiations? Coercive bargaining still involves a reconciliation of conflicting interests between parties. But one key difference between this kind of negotiation and traditional deal-making is that not all of the parties involved come to the table of their own volition, as the sisters did in the above example. Despite the fact that the sisters did not "maximize value"—i.e. they did not divide the orange in such a way as to maximize enjoyment for each girl— they both wanted to negotiate the division of the orange. In coercive bargaining, party A, unhappy with the status quo, forces party B to negotiate in order to persuade party B to accept a change to the status quo. In nuclear negotiations, for example, the United States is unhappy with the fact that Iran is developing a nuclear-weapons program and is forcing Iran to negotiate with the goal of having Tehran allay the suspicions (in Washington and around the world) that the Islamic Republic is seeking to acquire the capability to build a nuclear bomb. The second key difference is that coercive negotiation is more likely to be characterized by the use of aggressive tactics, such as threats.

In international politics, coercive bargaining (sometimes called coercive diplomacy) occupies the middle ground between diplomacy and war. It involves efforts by one state to change the behavior of another through military or economic threats and sanctions, as well as targeted, limited uses of military force and cyber capabilities. Such forceful negotiation tactics are attractive tools of statecraft because they hold out the promise of achieving tough geopolitical objectives—ones that purely diplomatic means are unable to attain— without resorting to full-scale military hostilities. As Sun Tzu writes in *The Art of War*, "To subdue the enemy without fighting is the acme of skill."

Key Advice for Teaching Negotiations
Emphasize Listening Skills and Empathy

"Leadership begins with listening," I often told students in the question-and-answer sessions at Handong Global University. In a negotiation, leadership means persuading people who do not initially believe that they should follow you to do so. This involves listening carefully, in order to understand why they feel the way they do. Only then is it possible to frame one's response around their concerns in a way that is likely to influence them.

Empathy, the ability to step into another person's shoes and understand that person's point of view, is a critical skill for successful negotiations. When one truly understands the other side's position and the feelings behind that position, one is better able to anticipate and respond to those feelings and concerns. Role-playing is an extremely effective way to build empathy. It is also an excellent example of experiential learning that, if well-prepared, forces the students to confront the complexity of a real-life situation.

The hamburger-spaghetti negotiation exercise in South Korea started with a simple task, in which students reflected and wrote down several views from both sides without knowing which side they would be asked to play in the role-play. One of the hamburger advocates told me with undisguised embarrassment that he could not help thinking like his colleague, who was arguing for eating spaghetti. I could not contain my excitement. "That is excellent," I exclaimed, "That is precisely the point!"—to build one's empathy to the point where you can think like the other person.

Directly Engage Students

In every class, I begin by asking students to create name cards so that we can call each other by name and begin building relationships. Recognizing that some students are naturally more comfortable speaking out than others, I make every attempt to solicit a wide variety of students' views. Indeed, I have found that students who rarely participate often make the most insightful contributions to class discussion, and many have indicated that they appreciate it when the instructor encourages their engagement in class.

After teaching in South Korea, I recognize even more clearly that by asking kids to engage, I am asking them to negotiate the relationship in the classroom by challenging the power structure that exists between a teacher and the student. It is one thing to tell students they are free to engage in bold, creative thinking and quite another to give them an example. Yet it is very important to do this explicitly. In South Korea, I asked the students to reflect on the importance of the platform at the front of the classroom. Why, I asked, is the platform important? What does it mean that the teacher is standing on the platform? How does it influence their learning? What is its significance? In a strictly hierarchical academic environment, these were tough question to raise. But by discussing an issue that was uncomfortable, I demonstrated that no issue was beyond the pale of classroom discussion.

The Setting Impacts the Negotiation

Most would agree that the context impacts the negotiation, but in practice too little attention is paid to these details. In order to get this idea across to students, I sometimes ask them to rearrange the room before we start. This pedagogical exercise gives students some owner-ship of their learning but also forces them to confront the question: how does the structure of the room matter in a negotiation?

Does it matter that people are negotiating across the table or sitting next to one another or conversing in a circle? If so, how? How might they describe the relationship between two parties facing one another across a table, as opposed to two parties sitting next to one another? What other room configurations are possible, and which will make a negotiation more likely to succeed or to founder?

Thinking about Teaching Style

In South Korea, I felt as if I had traveled back to my native Russia, where students were taught to memorize facts and respect their teach-ers but not to challenge them. Teaching in South Korea was thus a special opportunity for me to apply experiences that I have accumu-lated over the years. Indeed, since the schools I attended in my native Russia did not encourage creative thinking, I now exhort my students to debate robustly and respectfully with their classmates, with the au-thors they read, and, above all, with their own assumptions. Leading negotiation classes in South Korea gave me the opportunity to put this philosophy into action: I was designing the curriculum, including case studies, role-plays and simulations, for students who were unac-customed to the active engagement that I practice in the classroom.

In order to overcome their reluctance, I strove to create a safe and inclusive environment in which students knew that there were "no stupid questions." A classroom should be a safe space in which to engage in critical thinking. If not in the classroom, where else will students have the opportunity to think freely, to question assumptions, and, perhaps most importantly, to make mistakes and learn from them? It is important that students feel able to disagree with one another, but it is also important that no one feels too intimidated to express opinions that fall outside of widely held views.

On one day in my class there was no participation at all. I was surprised because I had explicitly told the students that they were free to make mistakes. "Why is this happening?" I asked my Korean-speaking teaching assistants. I was shocked to learn that because of a mistranslation, the impact of my message was the opposite of what I intended it to be. The students had understood me to say that "There should be no stupid questions in class." Whoops—I had done exactly what I wanted to avoid! After clutching my head in astonishment, I asked my Student Leaders to explain to the students in Korean the true meaning of my exhortation. The class slowly warmed up and comments flowed—gradually.

Why Teach Negotiation?

Why teach negotiating skills to young people? There are three main reasons. First, negotiating skills are important for future policy-makers and those who hope to impact their governments. Youth protests are now roiling in Hong Kong, and one of the protest leaders, seventeen-year-old Joshua Wong said, "I have no problems with negotiating…but before doing that, you better have some bargaining chips. If you don't have that, how do you fight a war?" I do not know if Joshua ever received formal negotiation training, but he had none-theless grasped one of its most important principles: developing lever-age means that your voice is more likely to be heard and that your demands are more likely to be accommodated.

Second negotiating skills help students resolve conflicts in mutually beneficial ways. In particular, they help students figure out how to develop creative compromises. That is because negotiation classes teach practical skills in listening more effectively to ideas with which they may not agree. In the process, they realize that underneath apparently opposing views there often lie core values that have more in common than the students originally realized. This is the essence of negotiation—finding commonalities in the fundamental "interests" that underlie the initial "positions" and thinking boldly about how to create solutions that will serve both sides. These are skill that South Korean high school students will need as they grow up and seek resolution and peace on the Korean peninsula.

Third, negotiating skills are practical. By learning to negotiate, students develop the ability to listen more effectively, to have difficult conversations with parents, friends, and colleagues more productive and less painful, and to build and sustain more successful relationships.

Conclusion: Teaching Negotiation to Young People

At a recent celebration of the Jewish Sabbath, a Harvard Rabbi told the congregation that people, especially scholars, who think constantly about complex issues run the risk of missing the simple yet fundamental topics. This was an important lesson from my teaching experience in South Korea: to understand negotiation, we must be able to teach it to young people. This often involves breaking down the complex ideas into seemingly basic activities, as in the "hamburgers or spaghetti" exercise. What may at first appear to be a simple classroom activity can provide an opportunity to develop creative solutions or spark a new interest that will lead students to deepen and expand their knowledge long after the workshop has ended.

A Sample Syllabus for a Negotia-tions Exercise

I have included a sample negotiations exercise so that readers interested in developing negotiations workshops have a sense of what they entail. In this example, I explain how I would teach an intensive executive education session on coercive negotiations.

The lecture in the first part of the session is devoted to an examination of the coercive-bargaining model, where leaders seek to translate actual military and economic power into leverage at an international negotiation table. The participants will consider how to systematically analyze their sources of leverage (military, economic, diplomatic, political); brainstorm their alternatives if coercive negotiation fails, as well as their options at the negotiation table, ranging from most desirable to minimally acceptable; shape the opponents' perceptions of their options at the negotiation table; create a unified domestic and international coalition in support of their policies; convey to the opponents the strongest possible perception of their own credibility; craft a strategy to confront and, if possible, divide and weaken the domestic and international coalitions of their opponents; and allow the opponents to back down while saving face.

During the exercise in the second part of the session, the participants can apply the above model to an ongoing coercive-bargaining situation—for example, the U.S.-Russia bargaining over Ukraine. Secretary of State John Kerry recently warned Russia that Moscow faced the prospect of tougher sanctions if it did not rein in the separatists in Eastern Ukraine. The participants will use this as a starting point for the exercise. Among the questions to be considered:

- What are the options for the U.S. if Russia does not back down, and what political challenges does the implementation of each of these measures present back in Washington? What responses are these tools likely to invite from the key decision-making factions in Moscow?
- What coercive leverage can Washington bring to bear on Russia while still leaving President Putin an "off ramp," as John F. Kennedy repeatedly did for Khrushchev in October 1962?
- What incentives can the United States offer to Russia, and to which domestic constituencies in Moscow will these offers most likely appeal?
- How does Moscow see the unfolding crisis?

At the beginning of the exercise, the class will divide into sets of Russian and American groups of two to four participants each. Each of the groups will prepare for a bilateral Russian-American negotiation by outlining each side's interests, allies, means of leverage (economic, military, and political), and options. The Russian and American groups will then convene for a first round of discussion with their respective peer groups (Russian with Russian, American with American)—a process that I will actively facilitate by helping each side work methodically through the above bullet points. Afterwards, I will lead a second round of discussion with the whole class in order to draw policy-relevant lessons for the current U.S.-Russian negotiations over Ukraine.

Chapter 9

Trilateral Leadership Summit:

Solving Asia's Tough Problems

John Lim

Yonsei/Fletcher, Harvard Extension School

● ● ●

Since 2014, I have been deeply involved in organizing a program called the Trilateral Leadership Summit (TLS), a program initiated by the Asia Leadership Institute (ALI) to provide high school students from China, Japan, and Korea with practical skills and knowledge to address the complexities of the trilateral relationship and develop collaborative solutions to promote cooperation among the three nations. The TLS is but one of the many programs organized by ALI to connect the vast educational resources at Harvard and Stanford with individuals and organizations in Asia who are working toward addressing key challenges facing the Asian continent.

The aim is to host TLS on a rotational basis among these three nations. The first program took place in November 2014 in Seoul, Korea. This second program was held in August 2015 in Sendai, Japan with the third one in Incheon, Korea in 2016. As of this writing, we are currently seeking to host the program in China. Having a successful turnout of the 2014 program with community support ramping up and representation from fourteen cities from these three countries, I had full confidence that this program was providing emerging leaders like our participants an ideal platform to define and manage a thought process and action plan of how Northeast Asia can gear up to make the region a better place for all to live, thrive, and flourish.

The TLS is facilitated by Teaching Fellows from the Harvard and Stanford communities. Over the years, we have had Fellows from twelve different countries who have shared their knowledge and expertise. During the program, Fellows provided participants opportunities to experience workshops on leadership, innovation, communication, and creativity. Fellows also facilitated seminars on career development, professional skills enhancement, and life skills coaching sessions with the participants. For Fellows, the TLS offered them the great opportunity to learn about Asia, through teaching, connecting and serving the local community.

This program was novel in its intention and approach from the start. Implementing change is not a task that can be accomplished easily. There are systemic and individual challenges such as policy reform, cultural barriers, and deep-rooted beliefs about history and identity, to name a few. Searching for answers to the question of "How will Asia's young people lead in the 21st century?" is a challenging task. In founding the Center for Asia Leadership Initiatives with my partner, Hungsoo S. Kim, who serves as President, we spent day and night debating on an effective model of education that can help young bright minds from these three countries to think and devise systems of cooperation or mechanisms of governance that can bring three critical nation states in Asia together.

This initiative was very important to Hungsoo and myself as we shared the ideals that the future of one's country and region lie in the hands of its young people. Opportunities for global leadership are plentiful in Northeast Asia as it has the potential to be the most prosperous region in the world. But the region also faces challenges due to geopolitical and strategic uncertainties surrounding its complex historical and territorial issues. Opportunities to convene young representatives from China, Japan, and Korea to participate in discussions, simulations, and skill-building workshops increase the chances for future leadership initiatives in the region, while offering a platform for inter-country dialogue, networking, awareness raising, and collaborative skill development.

One of the critical factors for success was that the program needed to acculturate participants away from a learning orientation that consisted of mere content mastery and information transfer. Instead, it needed to be a platform that could help delegates think independently and collaboratively to create solutions. Using the Harvard Kennedy School framework of 'Adaptive Leadership' and the 'Design Thinking' problem-solving approach popularized by institutions like the Stanford Design School and such firms as IDEO – the program was a testing ground of the relevance of emerging models of leadership and innovation training in an Asian context.

Harvard Kennedy School's 'Adaptive Leadership'

Developed in the 1980s by Ronald Heifetz of the Harvard Kennedy School, a key tenet of the 'Adaptive Leadership' framework is that leadership is not the same as management or authority. In some cases, making progress could actually be easier with a lower level of authority. Individuals with high levels of authority are often constrained by the demands of their own constituents. In the case of relations between China, Japan, and Korea, solutions to improving relations remain hard-pressed to come by from its political leaders. In Japan, conservative factions constrain Prime Minister Shinzo Abe from making progress on this problem. Although these factions share most of the blame in causing the problem, factions in China and Korea also impede cooperation. To make progress, those in positions of high authority would have to disappoint the expectations of those who actually authorized them in the first place. Exercising leadership would require them to go beyond their scope of authority. Solutions will necessarily have to also come from business, civil society, and in our program, students themselves.

When I led a discussion with a group of Chinese students analyzing the distinction between leadership and authority, I realized that the measures in which they evaluated "good leadership" in their country, was less on charisma or high-ranking authority and more on the ability of the leader to be forthright about a problem and in helping stakeholders play a part in advancing the solution. Indeed, China is at an inflection point in which its population needs to play a more active part in tackling its major challenges such as government corruption, environmental degradation, and social decay through hyper-consumerism.

Stanford's 'Design Thinking' Framework

The 'Design Thinking' workshop posed this problem to student delegates: "Today, ties between China, Japan, and Korea continue to strengthen. However, there are a number of issues that impede progress of cooperation. How might we strengthen ties between China, Japan, and Korea to facilitate strong economic, political, and cultural integration for further cooperative growth throughout Asia?"

Student delegates from each of the three countries engaged in interview sessions, with the aim of deeply understanding the other countries' perspectives on what obstructs cooperation. From that common database, they developed creative prototypes: a think tank funded by private donors and forward-thinking companies (from all three countries) that provides news and analysis that supports the obvious economic, business, and societal case for promoting cooperation; a Friendship Day celebrated by trilateral youth associations that are engaged in politics, diplomacy, and international exchange – which would partake in cultural activities as well as honor comfort women and victims of the war from each side; a standardized textbook written in three languages without government interference, that would clearly present the differences between the three perspectives but would aim to develop a nuanced view of why they are different; lastly, a museum that would be jointly developed by forward-thinking academics that would enable visitors to experience the lives of regular individuals from each of the three countries during the War.

Elements of Quality Teaching and Learning

Reflecting on student results from this program, another takeaway is a reaffirmation of the universal applicability of essential elements of quality teaching and learning (which is present in all of our Center's programs). One may be theoretically proficient in powerful frameworks such as 'Adaptive Leadership' or 'Design Thinking,' but if you are poor in facilitiating learning experiences with those frameworks, then the experience is utterly useless for your student. At the end of the day, an effective instructor delivers a transformative learning experience.

Admittedly, participants are usually drawn to our programs because of our Teaching Fellows and professors' affiliation with such institutions as Harvard. But what do people know about Harvard? Harvard has a track record of equipping its students for the future – for those with the confidence, skills, and mindsets to lead change. For starters, Harvard has produced forty-seven Nobel laureates, thirty-two heads of state, and forty-eight Pulitzer prize winners. Harvard living alums also happened to have founded 146,629 for profit and non-profit ventures accounting for a combined yearly revenue of USD 3.9 trillion, more than the GDP of Germany.

However, what matters fundamentally in a quality education is the quality of teaching and learning that can prepare one for the future. What can be easily practiced in Cambridge, Massachusetts, can be practiced in Beijing, Seoul, or Tokyo.

Let us take a look at four essential elements of quality teaching and learning.

Case

Using a broad definition of "case," a case is any problem or challenge that is able to connect the classroom to real life. Our experience of life is not mathematical, scientific, or artistic, per se. Instead we experience it as an integrated whole. Cases are simulations, projects, and meaningful discussions that create learning environments that simulate the world as it is: complex and multi-layered.

Reflection-in-Action

Secondly, learning experiences require reflection activities for the purpose of helping individuals develop a continuous learning mindset. We don't learn from experience – we learn from reflecting on experience. We do this by creating safe environments where students are challenged with continuous feedback and can honestly reflect on "failures" in the process of solving problems.

Smart Questions

Thirdly, students need to be taught the skill of asking smart questions, with the goal of independently solving new and complex problems. In order to gain perspective on a problem, you need to look at it from all angles. One example is the "IDEAS" framework: you begin with Identify (Observation), next is DE-brief (Different than expectations?), then Analyze (What were the reasons?), and finally Strategize (What do you want to happen next?) the steps in solving a problem.

Group Learning

Lastly, activities that provide platforms for group learning are needed. These allow students to learn how to build trust and create value with others. Individuals are trained to create greater value with others through collaborations rather than on an individual basis. Mechanisms in the classroom need to be set up that help individuals operate responsibly, productively, and respectfully in a democratic environment.

A New Level of Thinking

Albert Einstein once said, "We cannot solve our problems with the same level of thinking that created them." For the world's most intractable problems, there are no quick fixes because the solutions simply do not yet exist. In the larger scheme of things, each of these nations will not prosper to its full potential without a warm peace that enables them to collaborate on the challenges that face their country, their region, and the world. But our program shows that through enabling diverse people to come together through powerful learning experiences – to exchange ideas, widen perspectives, and take leadership initiatives – new thinking and creative solutions are indeed possible.

| Editors' Acknowledgments |

• • •

The editors of this book and the Asia Leadership Trek would like to extend our gratitude to the many people who made the Asia Leadership Trek 2015 and ALT V a reality.

To the ALT 2015 Trekkers, with whom we spent an unforgettable time traveling, learning, working, playing across Asia and in the process becoming lifelong friends: Co-organizers Jiro Yoshino, Andi Sparringa, Ng Beng Lean, Neha Sharma, Rajat Sethi, Sujit Thapa and Niranjan Khatri, and Trekkers Susanne Schwarz, Javier Fuentes, Nawal Lyana Binti Nafiz, Ahava Silkey-Jones, Fayrouz Saad, Cedrick Jones, Clara Carolina De Sa, Claude Al Tabar, Caitlin Callahan, Santhi Suppiah, Abdulaziz Said, Katherine Sooah Cho, Alanna Hughes, Aviva Feuerstein, Parul Batra, Emily Kunz, Bryant Renaud, Vivian Yuhang Wang, Francesca Ioffreda, Elizabeth Peyton, Simon Malian, Taniel Chan, Adauto Modesto Junior, Vincent Lampone, Rohit Sudarshan, Jooyeon June Koo, David Rose, Joseph Sakran, Rafael Rivera, Shruthi Saravanan, Joel Burns, Kaihan Yang, Tan Li Jean, Cathy Guo, Rachel Mason, Raghav Goel, Alison Flint and Joel Smoot.

To the ALT V Trekkers, with equal heart of gratitudes to our great friends: co-organizers John Lim, Jeff Chen, Marina Chan, Pitichoke

Chulapamornsri, Sirin Akaraphan, Oyunerdene Luvsannamsrai, Khongorzul Bat-Ireedui, and Zolbayar Jargalsaikhan, and Trekkers Annika Lawrence, Adam Malaty-Uhr, Amy Choi, Yingxin Wang, Caitlin Hartman, Masoomeh Khandan, Annie Yu Kleiman, Zolbayar Jargalsaikhan, Mahfuzul Islam, Ting Chen, Katie Mulroy, Sirin Akaraphan, Aaron Kleiman, Gregoire Jayot, Greg Manne, Lisa Marie Gomez, John Lim, Rachel Roberts, Ofir Zigelman, Marina Chan, Hany Beshr, Jeff Chen, Khongorzul Bat-Ireedui, Anna Stansbury, Nourhan Beshr, Chaitanya Kansal, Pitichoke Chulapamornsri, Jiro Yoshino, Simon Mueller, Evelien Blom, Taeko Kohara, Dulguun Bayasgalan, John Lee, Clare Claro, Oyunerdene Luvsannamsrai, Anji Sauve Clubb, and Kevin Tan.

To the Asia Center of Harvard University which supported us, believed in our idea and provided advice in both our formative and our execution stages.

To the Professors and staff at the Harvard University who graciously offered their instruction, advice, and mentorship to the Asia Leadership Trek: Professor Arthur Kleinman, Professor Jay Rosengard, and Mr. Jon Mills.

For both the ALT 2015 and ALT V, our sincere gratitude goes to the following individuals and organizations for sharing their invaluable time and insights with us:

In the Philippines, the Honorable Speaker Feliciano Belmonte, Jr., Hon. Giorgidi B. Aggabao, Deputy Speaker; Hon. Roman T. Romulo, Chairman, Committee on Higher Technical Education; Hon. Kimi S. Cojuango, Chairperson, Committee on Basic Education & Culture; Hon. Hon Rufus B. Rodriguez, Chairman, Ad Hoc Committee on Bangsamoro Basic Law; Hon. Jim Hayaman-Salliman,

Chairman, Committee on Peace Reconciliation and Unity; Hon. Anthony G. Del Rosario, Chairman, Committee on Youth & Sports Development, Hon. Mercedes K. Alvarez, Vice Chairperson, Committee on Appropriations; Hon. Dakila Carlo E. Cua, Vice Chairman, Committee on Globalization & WTO; Hon. Ferdinand G Romualdez, member, Committee on Appropriations; Hon. Terry L. Ridon, member, Committee on Higher & Technical Education; the Philippine House of Congress; Philip Goldberg, the U.S. Ambassador to the Philippines; Mr. Butch Abad, Chairman of the Ayala Group; the Ministry of Foreign Affairs; Former Education Secretary; Ms. Pia Hontiveros, SM Investment Group and SM Foundation; Mr. Jaime Zobel de Ayala, CNN Correspondent; the Asian Development Bank; the Harvard Club of the Philippines; and the GMA 7 Network.

In Indonesia, Honorable Jusuf Kalla, Vice President of Indonesia; Dr. Darmansjah Djumala, Head of Policy Analysis and Development Agency, Ministry of Foreign Affairs; Dr. Dino Patti Djalal, Foreign Policy Community Indonesia and Diaspora Indonesia; Mr. Sutanto Hartono, CEO of SCTV, Mr. Hilmi Panigoro and Mr. Arie Ariotedjo from PT Medco Energi Internasional; Mr. John Riady, CEO of Lippo Group; the Yayasan KDM (Kampus Diakonia Modern); Ms. Putri Kuswisnuwardarni, Chairlady and four Miss Indonesia of the Taman Sari Royal Heritage Spa Jakarta; members of the Indonesian Young Entrepreneurs Club (HIPMI), Mr. Hasyim Djojohadikusomo, a renowned and highly respected entrepreneur.

In Malaysia, Senator Idris Jala, Minister in the Prime Minister's Department and CEO of PEMANDU; Senator Paul Low, Minister in the Prime Minister's Department; Honorable Khairy Jamaluddin, Minister of Youth and Sports; Dr. Jeffrey Cheah, Founder and Chairman of Sunway Group; Dr. Lin See-Yan, President of the Harvard Club of Malaysia; Ms. Sarena Cheah, Director of Strategic and Corporate Development at Sunway City Berhad; Mr. Evan Cheah, Executive Vice President, President's Office and Chief Executive Officer, Sunway China; Dr. Lee Weng Keng, CEO of Education and Healthcare Division of Sunway Group; Dr. Elizabeth Lee, Senior Executive Director of Sunway Education Group; Ms. Ng Beng Lean, Director of Senior Executive Director's Office, Sunway Education Group; Mr. Wong Wan Wooi, Ms. Nolee Ashilin Mohammed Radzi, Perak State Exco for Tourism, Art and Culture, Dr. Mazalan Kamis, CEO of IDR, Perak Institute Darul Ridzuan, H.R.H. Sultan Nazrin Shah, Sultan of Perak, Prof Jorge I.Dominguez, Vice Provost for International Affairs, Harvard Alumni Association Networking Dinner, Deputy Chief of Mission, Mr. Edgard Kagan of the Malaysian-American Commission on Education Exchange, H.E. Ambassador Joseph Y. Yun, Embassy of the USA, Mr. Meer Sadik Habib, Managing Director of Habib Jewels, Mr. Yong Poh Kon, Royal Selangor Pewter, School of Hard Knocks, Mr. Abdul Farid Alias, Group President & Chief Executive Officer, Malayan Banking Bhd, Mr. Wong Chun Wai, CEO, Ms. Leanne Goh, Group Chief Editor, Ms. June Wong, COO, Content Development, Mr. M. Shanmugam, specialist editor – Business, Ms. Maryann Tan, GM, Corporate Planning and Strategy, Ms. Ivy Soon, editor – Women & Family, of The Star.

In China, Stars Youth Development Center, Dajiang Innovation, Tencent Corporation, Qianhai Free Trade Zone, and China-Hong Kong Entrepreneurs Academy as well as six public universities and high schools.

In Hong Kong, Mr. Lam Kin Chung, Chairman of Zhong Yang

Group Holdings Ltd and Chairman of the Lam Kin Chung Morning Sun Charity Fund; the Swire Properties - Blueprint Project; InvestHK, Hong Kong Council of Social Service, the Legislative Council Education Constituency; the Harvard Club of Hong Kong; the Social Ventures of Hong Kong; the Asia Miles; the Diamond Cab; and the Cathay Pacific Innovation Centre.

In Thailand, Dr. Mechai Viravaidya, former Deputy Minister of Industry also known as the "Condom King;" the Bank of Thailand; Dr. Kriengsak Chareonwongsak, a renowned scholar and a politician; the CP Group, the nation's representative conglomerate; International Labor Organization; Stock Exchange of Thailand (SET); HUBBA (Thailand Startup Incubator); and the Teach For Thailand.

In Korea, Chairwoman of the Foreign Affairs and Unification Committee of the National Assembly of the Republic of Korea, Representative Na Kyung-won; Dr. In-Chul Kim, President of the Hankuk University of Foreign Studies; Kim & Chang, especially Mr. Young Joon Mok, Chairman of the Committee for Social Contribution and also a former Justice of the Constitutional Court of the Republic of Korea, and Ms. Minjo Kim, an attorney; Former MP Park Jin, and Dr. Michael L. McManus of Hankuk University of Foreign Studies; WCO Korea; the Korea Tourism Organization, Teach North Korea; Mr. Jinok Heo, CEO of ISM, a rising Social Enterprise and Human & Economy Foundation, the Nanta performers, and Odusan Unification Observatory.

In Mongolia, the Honorable Chimed Saikhanbileg, Prime Minister, Mr Zandaakhuu Enkhbold, Speaker of the Parliament; Oyu Tolgoi, Mayor of Ulaanbaatar, Governor of the Central Bank and the Executive Excellence Center; Ministry of Mining; Ministry of Tourism; Harvard Club.

In Japan, Mr. Kuwajim, an Economist on "Abenonomics;" Japan Olympic Center; and Biz Japan.

In India, Mr. Shri Pranab Mukherjee, President; Mr. Shri Jayant Sinha, Minister of State of Finance; Ms. Smriti Zubin Irani, Minister of Human Resource & Development; Minister of IT & Communications; Mr. Raghuram Rajan, Governor of the Reserve Bank of India; Mr. Naveen Jindal, owner and CEO of Jindal Steel and Power Ltd. Plant; Apeejay University, School of Management; and Tata Company at Bombay House.

In Nepal, Ms. Chitra Lekha Yadab, Minister of Education; Dr. Govinda Pokharel, Vice Chancellor of the National Planning Commission; Mr. Pradeep Shrestha of Panchakanya Steels and Previous Chairman of Federation of Nepal Chambers of Commerce and Industries; Mr. Gagan Kumar Thapa, MP of Nepal's Constituent Assembly; Mr. Arjun Narasingha KC, MP of Nepal Constituent Congress; Dr. Narayan Narsingh Khatri, Development Economics Professor; Indira, PA Nepal Chairman, Mr. Ajit Narayan Singh Thapa's Residence; the Nepal Tourism Board; Professors at the Kathmandu University; and Entrepreneurs' Organization.

Thank you for all your hard work, support and leadership.

| Appendix I |
Trek and Fellowship Itinerary

• • •

Asia Leadership Fellowship 2015

Date	Events
January 5 – 7	**Asia Leadership Boot Camp** A Capacity Building Program for Social Leaders Seoul, Korea
January 12 – 16	**Asia Leadership Youth Camp** Making of a Leader Pohang, Korea
January 17	**Asia Leadership Conference 2015** Developing Forefront and Cutting-Edge Asian Leaders in the 21st Century Manila, Philippines
January 19 – 21	**Asia Leadership Boot Camp** Developing Forefront and Cutting-Edge Asian Leaders in the 21st Century Manila, Philippines
July 3 – 5	**Emerging Leaders Program for Youth** Leaders in Development Ho Chi Minh City, Vietnam
July 7	**Asia Leadership Summer School** Art and Practice of Leadership Development Gongju, Korea

Date	Event
July 13 – 17	**Asia Leadership Summer School** Developing Heart, Mind and Skills for Effective Leadership Beijing, China
July 20 – 24	**Asia Leadership Youth Camp 2015** Values into Action Kuala Lumpur, Malaysia
July 27 – 31	**Executive Leadership School 2015** Redefining Success Kuala Lumpur, Malaysia
August 3 – 7	**One Korea, One Nation** The Nexus for the Young Leaders Towards the Nation's Reunification Seoul, Korea
August 10 – 12	**Asia Leadership Summer School: Youth** Leaders in Development Guangzhou, China
August 13 – 15	**Asia Leadership Summer School: Young Professionals** Art and Practice of Leadership Development Guangzhou, China
August 17 – 21	**Trilateral Leadership Summit II** Working Towards the Thriving Northeast Asia Sendai, Japan

●●●

Asia Leadership Trek 2015

Sunday, December 28

6:00pm	Arrival in Tokyo from Boston Check-in at Japan Olympic Center
8:00pm	Welcoming Dinner at Shibuya

Monday, December 29

9:00am – 1:00pm	**Asia Leadership Conference 2015 in Tokyo**
9:00am	Welcoming Speech by Hungsoo S. Kim, President of Asia Leadership Trek (ALT)
9:15am	Forum Discussion on 'Creating an Impact through Walking-the Talk Leadership' by Taniel Chan (US, HBS MBA), Susanne Schwarz (Germany, HKS MPP), Neha Sharma (India, HKS MPA), Katherine Cho (Korea, HKS MPP & HBS MBA), and Claude Al Tabar (Lebanon, HKS MPAID), moderated by Ryosuke Tane, Consultant at Bain Capital Tokyo
10:00am	Special Talk by Tan Li Jean (Malaysia, Sunway), Shruthi Saravanan (India, HGSE Ed.M.), Rafael Fuentes (Mexico, HBS MBA)
10:40am	Workshop Sessions on Leading with Passion by Santhi Suppiah (Malaysia, Sunway), Decision Making by David Rose (US, HBS MBA), Cross Cultural Communication: Embracing Others and Debunking Stereotypes by Rachel Mason (US, HGSE Ed.M), Design Thinking by Alanna Hughes (US, MIT MBA & HKS MPA), and Persuasion by Aviva Feuerstein (US, HKS MPP)
12:00pm	Networking Event
1:00pm	Closing Remarks by Hungsoo S. Kim, President of ALT

1:30pm	Sightseeing of Tokyo Group 1: Tokyo Imperial Palace, Otemosando, and Shinjuku Group 2: Roppongi, Obaida, Tokyo Tower, Senso-ji, and Harajuku Group 3: Yoyogi Park, Shinjuku, and Tokyo National Museum Group 4: Kaminarimon, Tokyo City View Sky Deck, Ginza, and Tokyo University

Tuesday, December 30

9:00am	Guided Tour of Meiji Jingu & Dialogue with Senior Management of the Shrine
3:00pm	Dialogue with Mr. Kuwajima on 'Diagnosis on the Abenomics'
4:30pm	Dialogue with Mr. Yoshimasa Hayashi, Member of the Parliament of Japan on 'Japan's Role in Asia'
7:00pm	Mixer with Japanese Entrepreneurs at Roppongi Hills

Wednesday, December 31

10:00am	Sightseeing of Hase Temple
11:00am	Tour of Kamakura, an Ancient City near Tokyo – Great Buddha of Kamakura
2:00pm	Tour of Yokohama China Town
7:00pm	Depart for Seoul

Thursday, January 1

9:00am	Sightseeing of Seoul Group 1: Myungdong, Gwanghwamun, Gyungbokgung, and Insadong Group 2: Bukchon, Gwangwhamun, Seoul City Hall, and Yongsan Group 3: Gangnam, Bongeunsa, Lotte World, and Olympic Park Group 4: Yeouido, National Museum of Korea, War Memorial, and 63 Building
4:00pm	Free & Rest Time
6:00pm	JUMP – Korean Martial Arts Comedy Show

| 8:00pm | New Year's Dinner at a Korean Traditional Restaurant |

Friday, January 2

8:30am	Dialogue with Senior Leadership of the Ruling Saenuri Party
10:30am	Guided Tour of the National Assembly of Korea
1:00pm	Lunch with President and Senior Leadership of Hankuk University of Foreign Studies
2:00pm	University Introduction by Dr. Michael L. McManus
2:30pm	Welcoming Speech by President Incheol Kim, Ph.D
2:40pm	Special Seminar by Dr. Park Jin on Korea in the 21st Century World
4:30pm	Campus Tour of HUFS
6:00pm	Special Session with the Teach North Korean Refugees
8:00pm	Taekwondo Learning Session

Saturday, January 3

| 9:00am | Organized Sightseeing of Seoul: Dongdaemun, Seoul Tower, and Yongsan Hot Springs |
| 3:00pm | Rest and Free Day |

Sunday, January 4

| 9:30am | Travel to Jakarta |

Monday, January 5

9:00am	Dialogue with the Head of Policy Analysis and Development Agency of Indonesian Ministry of Foreign Affairs
10:30am	Dialogue with Dr. Dino Patti Djalal, President of Foreign Policy Community Indonesia and Diaspora Indonesia, Former Vice Minister of Foreign Affairs, Former Ambassador of Indonesia to US, and Former Presidential Spokesperson
2:00pm	Guided Tour of SCTV and Dialogue with Sutanto Hartono, CEO and Senior Executives

| 4:00pm | Company Tour of Tiket.com and Presentation by Jonathan Sariaatmadja, CEO and Head Engineers |
| 6:00pm | Company Visit to PT Medco Energi International & Dialogue with Hilmi Panigoro, President Director and Mr. Arie Ariotedjo, Managing Director and other Senior Leaders |

Tuesday, January 6

10:30am	Campus Tour of Universitas Pelita Harapan
12:00pm	Lunch with Senior Leaders of UPH
1:00pm – 4:30pm	**Asia Leadership Conference 2015 in Jakarta**
1:00pm	Welcome Remarks by Dean of UPH School of Political Sciences and Communication Studies, Professor Aleksius Jemadu, Ph.D.
1:10pm	Opening by Hungsoo S. Kim, President of ALT
1:20pm	Panel Session on 'Creating Shared Values on Leadership' by Taniel Chan (US, HBS MBA), Francesca Ioffreda (US, HBS MBA), Abdulaziz Said (US, HKS MPP), and Parul Batra (India, MIT MBA)
2:20pm	Tea Break & Networking Session
2:40pm	Workshop Breakout Session on Persuasion: Everyday Exercise to Rally Opinions, Social Entrepreneurship: From Idea to Realization, Career at an International Organization, Becoming a Foreign Service Official, and Working at a Consulting Firm
4:20pm	Closing Remarks by Hungsoo S. Kim, President of ALT
5:40pm	Dialogue with John Riady, Director of the Lippo Group
7:00pm	Community Service Event and Cultural Night at Yayasan Kampur Diakonia Modern Indonesia with Special Music Performance by Mesty Ariotedjo

Wednesday, January 7

| 10:00am | Guided Tour of the Jakarta Regional House of Representatives (DPRD DKI) and Dialogue with the Vice Governor of DKI, Basuki Tjahaja Purnama |
| 12:00pm | Luncheon with Senior Leaders of DPRD DKI |

2:00pm	Meeting with Mustika Ratu & Dialogue on Indonesian Beauty Culture
3:00pm	Dialogue with Miss Indonesia
4:00pm	Javanese Massage
6:00pm	Hosted Dinner with Indonesian Young Entrepreneurs Club (HIPMI) & Dialogue with the Senior Leadership

Thursday, January 8

9:00am	Dialogue with Puan Maharani, Minister of Human Development and Cultural Affairs
2:00pm	Dialogue with Hashim Djojohadikusomo, former President and Chairman of the Board of CITIC Canada Petroleum, on the Future of the Indonesian Democracy and Economic Development
5:00pm	Sightseeing of Jakarta: National Monument, Istiqlal Mosque and National Museum of Indonesia
9:00pm	Travel to Kuala Lumpur

Friday, January 9

9:00am	Tour of the Sunway Township
10:00am	Presentation of Sunway Resort City and Sunway City Ipoh
11:00am	Panel Discussion on 'Sustainability and Livability'
12:00pm	Luncheon with Sunway Group Board Members
3:00pm	Guided Tour of the Federal Government Administrative Center
3:30pm	Roundtable Meeting with Honorable Minister Paul Low in the Prime Minister's Department on "Issues and Challenges of Good Governance in Malaysia"
4:30pm	Briefing on the National Government and Economic Transformation Programs
5:00pm	Dialogue with Honorable Minister Idris Jala in the Prime Minister's Department and CEO of PEMANDU on "Malaysia's Social, Economic & Political Transformation in the 21st Century"
8:00pm	Conference Preparatory Meeting

Saturday, January 10

9-5pm	**Asia Leadership Conference 2015 in Kuala Lumpur**
8:30am	Registration
9:00am	Opening Remarks by Hungsoo S. Kim, President of ALT
9:10am	Welcoming Speech by Dr Elizabeth Lee Senior Executive Director of Sunway Education Group
9:15am	Keynote Address by Honorable Minister Youth and Sports, Khairy Jamaluddin Abu Bakar
10:15am	Tea Break & Networking Session
10:30am	Special Talk on the Importance of Humility in Leadership by Parul Batra (India, MIT MBA)
10:45am	Forum Discussion on 'From Good Intention to Leading Social Change' by Bryant Renaud (US, HKS MPP), and Fayrouz Saad (US, HKS MCMPA)
11:15am	Workshop Breakout Session 1
12:35pm	Lunch
1:30pm	Special Talk on 'Realizing the Potential of Your Profession' by Joseph Sakran (US, HKS MCMPA)
1:50pm	Workshop Breakout Session 2
3:10pm	Tea Break & Networking Session
3:30pm	Career Mentoring and Professional Skills Development Session
4:30pm	Special Talk on 'Science Policy in the US: Global Leader, Domestic Debate' by Joel Smoot (US, HKS MPP)
4:45pm	Closing Remarks by Professor Graeme Wilkinson, Vice-Chancellor of Sunway University
6:00pm	Rest & Free Time

Sunday, January 11

9:00am	Sightseeing of Kuala Lumpur: Merdeka Square, KL Tower, National Museum, Bukit Bintang, Batu Caves, National Mosque of Malaysia, and Petronas Twin Towers

Monday, January 12

7:00am	Travel to Ipoh, Perak
10:00am	Breakfast Hosted by Sunway City Ipoh

11:00am	Corporate Presentation by Mr. Wong Wan Wooi, Director Sunway Ipoh
12:00pm	Guided Tour of Ipoh City
2:30pm	Tour of Lost World of Tambun & the Banjaran Hot Springs Resort
5:00pm	Guided Tour of Kellie's Night Castle
7:00pm	Dinner with Board Members of Perak State for Tourism, Art and Culture, Nolee Ashilin and Mohammed Radzi

Tuesday, January 13

9:00am	Explore 6th Mile Cave
12:00pm	Lunch Hosted by Lost World of Tambun
2:30pm	Forum with Perak Institute Darul Ridzuan (IDR) on 'Leapfrogging to a High Income State: Opportunities and Challenges for Perak'
4:30pm	Special Presentation by Dr. Mazalan Kamis, CEO of IDR
7:00pm	Tea & Networking Session with Local Community Leaders
8:00pm	Cocktail Reception
10:00pm	Dinner with Guest of Honor, HRH Nazrin Shah, Sultan of Perak and Professor. Jorge I. Dominguez, Vice Provost for International Affairs of Harvard University Welcome Speech by Dr. Jeffrey Cheah, Founder and Chairman of Sunway Group

Wednesday, January 14

9-2pm	**Asia Leadership Conference 2015 in Ipoh**
10:00am	Opening Remarks by Hungsoo S. Kim, President of ALT
10:10am	Welcoming Speech by Dr. Elizabeth Lee, Sunway Education Group
10:15am	Forum Discussion on 'Social Change Agent: Roles and Responsibilities' by Taniel Chan (US, HBS MBA), Joel Burns (US, HKS MCMPA), Ahava Silkey-Jones (US, HGSE Ed.M.), and Aviva Feuerstein (US, HKS MPP)

11:00am	Special Talk on 'Overcoming Adversities in Life' by David Rose (HKS MPP & HBS MBA)
11:20am	Workshop Breakout Session
12:40pm	Career Mentoring & Professional Skills Development Sessions
1:20pm	Special Talk on 'Redefining Village for the Contemporary Urban Professional' by Alanna Hughes (US, MIT MBA)
1:35pm	Closing Remarks by Cheng Mien Wee, Executive Director of Sunway College Ipoh
4:30pm	Travel to Kuala Lumpur
8:00pm	Harvard Alumni Association Networking Dinner Hosted by the Harvard Club of Malaysia

Thursday, January 15

9:30am	Meeting with the Malaysian-American Commission on Education Exchange (MACEE) &
10:00am	Roundtable Discussion with the Deputy Chief of Mission, Edgard Kagan, on "Malaysia and Asia in the 21st Century"
10:30am	Courtesy Call on H.E. Ambassador Joseph Y. Yun, Embassy of the USA
11:30am	Guided Tour of Habib Jewels Headquarters
12:30pm	Luncheon with Managing Director of Habib Jewels, Meer Sadik Habib, on "Building a Malaysian Brand into a Global Brand"
3:00pm	Tour of Royal Selangor Museum showing Tin Mining & Early Pewter
3:30pm	Dialogue with Yong Poh Kon, CEO of Royal Selangor Pewter, on "Improving Malaysia's Competitiveness in the 21st Century"
4:00pm	Factory Tour & School of Hard Knocks
7:30pm	Forum Hosted by Abdul Farid Alias, Group President & CEO of Maybank Corporation
9:00pm	Dinner with Senior Management of Maybank

Friday, January 16

11:00am	Tour of The Star Gallery and Editorial Floors
11:30am	Forum with Wong Chun Wai, Group Managing Director and CEO, Leanne Goh, Group Chief Editor, June Wong, COO, Content Development, M. Shanmugam, Specialist Editor of Business, Maryann Tan, GM, Corporate Planning and Strategy, and Ivy Soon, Editor of Women & Family
1:30pm	Networking Lunch Hosted by The Star
6:00pm	Travel to Mumbai

Saturday, January 17

10:30am	Guided Tour of the Bollywood Complex
11:30am	Meeting with Senior Management of Yashraj Films
4:00pm	Dialogue with Governor of Reserve Bank of India, Raghuram Rajan
5:30pm	Sightseeing of Dadar Flower Market and Chor Bazaar
6:30pm	Dialogue with Dr. NR Rajan, Director of Human Resources, and Dr. Mukund Rajan, Member of Group Executive Council of Tata Sons at Bombay House

Sunday, January 18

9:00am	Free Time Group 1: Reality Tours of India Slums Group 2: Sightseeing of Mumbai: Gateway of India, Chhatrapati Shivaji Terminus Railway Station, Haji Ali Dargah
9:00pm	Travel to New Delhi

Monday, January 19

6:00am	Travel to Odisha
9:00am	Guided Tour of Jindal Steel and Power Plant in Angul
10:30am	Dialogue with Naveen Jindal, Owner and CEO of Jindal Steel Group

11:30am	Presentation on Corporate Sustainability
4:00pm	Travel to New Delhi Tour of Qutub Minar, Humayun's Tomb, and Red Fort Tour of Delhi Haat Dinner at HauzKhas Village

Tuesday, January 20

10:00am – 1:00pm	**Asia Leadership Conference 2015 in New Delhi at Apeejay University**
10:00am	Opening Remarks by Hungsoo S. Kim, President of ALT
10:10am	Welcoming Speech by Smt. Sushma Paul Berlia, President, Apeejay Education Society and Co - Founder & Chancellor, Apeejay Stya University
10:20am	Keynote Speech by Shri Vijay Berlia, General Secretary of Apeejay Education Society, on 'Future of India'
10:50am	Workshop Breakout Session on Leadership and Identity, Cross-Cultural Communications: Embracing Other and Debunking Stereotypes, Entrepreneurship in Developing World, Improving Communication Skills: Interviews, and Social Media: How to make or Break Your Life
12:30pm	Closing Remarks by Dr. Alok Saklani, Director of School of Management
3:00pm	Dialogue with Honorable Minister of Human Resource & Development, Smrithi Irani
4:00pm	Shopping at a Local Flea Market
6:00pm	Reception & Dinner at Apeejay University

Wednesday, January 21

9:00am	Roundtable Discussion with Honorable Minister of IT & Communications of India, Ravi Shankar Prasad
10:30am	Sightseeing of Old Delhi and Humayun's Tomb
2:30pm	Roundtable Discussion with Honorable Minister of State for Finance of India, Jayant Sinha
5:00pm	Farewell Dinner & Party

Thursday, January 22

| 8:00am | Optional Tour to Taj Mahal, Agra |
| 8:00pm | Departure for Boston |

Friday, January 23

6:00am	Departure for Kathmandu, Nepal for an Optional Trek
12:00pm	Campus Tour of the Kathmandu University
1:00pm – 4:30pm	**Asia Leadership Conference 2015 in Kathmandu for Faculty at Kathmandu University**
1:00pm	Opening Remarks by Hungsoo S. Kim, President of ALT
1:10pm	Welcoming Speech by Professor Dr. Ram Kantha Makaju Shrestha, Vice-Chancellor of Kathmandu University
1:20pm	Special Talk by Aviva Feuerstein (US, HKS MPP)
1:40pm	Workshop Breakout Session on Leadership and Identity, Cross-Cultural Communications: Embracing Other and Debunking Stereotypes, Entrepreneurship in Developing World, and Adaptive Leadership
3:00pm	Reception
4:00pm	Dialogue with Professor Dr. Ram Kantha Makaju Shrestha, Vice-Chancellor of Kathmandu University
5:00pm	Travel to Nagarkot

Saturday, January 24

7:00am	Hiking Walk around Nagarkot & Enjoying the View of the Himalayas
8:30am	Tour of the Bhutapar
10:00am	Tour of Patan
12:00pm	Dialogue with Dr. Govinda Pokharel, Vice Chancellor of the National Planning Commission
2:30pm	Dialogue with Pradeep Shrestha, President of Panchakanya Steels and Former Chairman of Federation of Nepal Chambers of Commerce and Industries

6:00pm	Dialogue with Anuradha Koirala, President of Maiti Nepal Networking Dinner with Entrepreneurs' Organization at Radisson Hotel
9:00pm	Welcome Party at Thamel

Sunday, January 25

7:30am	Dialogue with Gagan Kumar Thapa, Member of Parliament of Nepalese Constituent Assembly
9:30am	Tour of Pashupunath, Cremation Site
11:30am	Luncheon with Arjun Narasingha KC, Member of Parliament of Nepal Constituent Congress, and Dr. Narayan Narsingh Khatri, Member of National Development Council
2:30pm	Dialogue with Indira Ranamagar, Chairman of Prisoner's Assistance Nepal
5:00pm	Dialogue with Army General, Rajendra Chhetri and Ajit Narayan Singh Thapa, President and a Director at Miteri Development Bank

Monday, January 26

9:00am	Dialogue with Honorable Minister of Education of Nepal, Chitra Lekha Yadav
11:00am	Visit to Nepal Tourism Board
11:30am – 4:30pm	**Asia Leadership Conference 2015 in Kathmandu at Nepal Tourism Board**
11:30am	Opening Remarks by Hungsoo S. Kim, President of Asia Leadership Trek
11:35pm	Welcoming Speech by Shankar Prasad Adhikari, Secretary at the Ministry of Tourism and Civil Aviation
11:40am	Special Talk by Simon Malian (Australia, Harvard FAS MA)
12:00pm	Workshop Sessions on Leadership and Identity, Cross-Cultural Communications: Embracing Other and Debunking Stereotypes, Entrepreneurship in Developing World, and Adaptive Leadership
1:30pm	Forum Discussion on 'Leadership and Innovation in Nepal'
2:30pm	Design Thinking and Innovation Workshop
4:00pm	Press Conference

7:00pm   Travel to Boston

● ● ●

Korea & Mongolia Leadership Trek

Saturday, March 14

    Arrival in Seoul from Boston

7:00pm   Welcome Dinner at Insadong

Sunday, March 15

9:00am   Sightseeing of Seoul: Gyungbokgung, Insadong, Seoul Tower, War Museum, National Museum, Sinsadong, Olympic Park and Gangnam

Monday, March 16

10:00am   Samsung Innovation Museum

1:00pm   DMZ – UNCMAC Presentation, Tour of OP Dora and Tunnel 3

7:40pm   Travel to Ulaan Baatar

11:00pm   Mongolian Welcome Ceremony

Tuesday, March 17

9:00am   Travel to Terelj Steppe

11:00am   Hiking and Horse Riding

6:00pm   Mongolian Feast

11:00pm   Overnight in the Ger

Wednesday, March 18

8:00am	Travel to Ulaan Baatar
10:00am	Ulaan Baatar Downtown Walking Tour
11:00am	Tour of the National Parliament Square and Group PictureBuilding & Museum
2:00pm	Meeting with Senior Management of Oyu Tolgoi
3:00pm	Dialogue with Honorable US Ambassador to Mongolia, Piper Campbell & Presentation by US Embassy on Geopolitics of Mongolia and Cultural Diplomacy
5:00pm	Dinner Meeting with Business Council of Mongolia and World Economic Forum Global Shapers

Thursday, March 19

9:00am	Dialogue with Matthieu Le Blan, Head of the European Bank for Reconstruction and Development Office of Mongolia on 'Opportunities and Challenges of Doing Business in Mongolia'
10:30am	Dialogue with Gerard Mestrallet, CEO of GDF Suez Mongolia on 'Mongolia's Energy Landscape and Market Development'
1:00pm	Dialogue with Honorable Minister of Mining Energy, Byanma Jigjid on 'Prospects of Energy Market Development in Mongolia'
2:30pm	Dialogue with Honorable Minister of Environment, Green Development and Tourism, D. Oyunkhorol on 'Government Measure to Promote Tourism Industry and Curbing Environmental Degradation
4:00pm	Campus Tour of the American School of Ulaanbaatar
4:30pm – 6:00pm	**Asia Leadership Conference 2015 in Ulaan Baatar at American School of Ulaanbaatar**
4:30pm	Opening Remarks by Hungsoo S. Kim, President of ALT
4:35pm	Welcoming Speech by Dr. Kate Sutton Jones, Secondary School Principal
4:40pm	Special Talk by Amy Wang (US, MIT MBA)
4:50pm	Panel Discussion on Leadership Practices & Preparing for US School Admissions by Soojin Park (Korea, Dartmouth BA), David Klausner (US, HKS MPP), Khongorzul Bat-Ireedui (Mongolia, Fletcher MALD), and Paola Cordovez (Ecuador, HKS MPP)
5:30pm	Q&A Session

| 6:30pm | Mixer with Harvard Alumni of Mongolia |
| 8:30pm | Networking Event with Junior Chamber International Members |

Friday, March 20

9:00am	Dialogue with Honorable Deputy Speaker of the Parliament, Miyeegombyn Enkhbold on 'Political History and Dynamics of Mongolia'
11:00am	Courtesy Call by Honorable President of Mongolia and HKS Alum, Tsakhiagiin Elbegdorj on 'Mongolia and the World in the 21st Century'
12:00pm	Group Picture and Exchange of Gifts
1:00pm	Tour of the Parliament and Parliament Museum
2:30pm	Dialogue with Honorable Deputy Minister of Foreign Affairs and a Member of Parliament, Navaan-Yundengiin Oyundari
4:00pm	Sightseeing of Ulaan Baatar: National Museum, Winter Palace of Bogd Khan and Choijin Lama Temple
8:00pm	Overnight Train to Erdenet

Saturday, March 21

| 8:00am | Tour of Erdenet |
| 6:00pm | Overnight Train back to Ulaan Baatar |

Sunday, March 22

9:00am	Tour of Gandan Monastery
11:00am	Tour of Zanabazar Museum
1:00pm	Luncheon with Honorable Deputy Prime Minister of Mongolia, Khurelsukh Ukhnaa
3:00pm	Dialogue with CEO of Khan Bank, Norihiko Kato
5:00pm	Free and Rest Time
11:50pm	Depart for Seoul

Monday, March 23

Travel to Boston

* * *

Asia Leadership Trek V

Thursday, June 4

	Arrival in Manila from Boston
8:00pm	Welcoming Dinner

Friday, June 5

10:30am	Dialogue with Honorable US Ambassador to the Philippines, Philip Goldberg
1:30pm	Dialogue with Senior Executives of the SM Investment Group and SM Foundation & Guided Tour of the Company Premise
4:00pm	ALT V Orientation

Saturday, June 6

8:00am – 1:00pm	**Asia Leadership Conference 2015 in Manila with SM Foundation**
8:00am	Registration
8:30am	Opening Remarks by Hungsoo S. Kim, President of ALT
8:35am	Welcoming Speech by Deborah Pe Sy, SM Foundation Executive Director
8:40am	Special Talk by Adam Malaty-Uhr (US, HGSE Ed.M.) and Katie Mulroy (US, HGSE Ed.M.)

9:10am	Forum Discussion on 'New Perspectives on Leadership and Innovation,' by Annika Lawrence (US, HGSE Ed.M.), Anna Stansbury (Great Britain, HKS MPA), Gregoire Jayot (France, HKS MPA), and Ofir Zigelman (Israel, HKS MPA) followed by Q&A Sessions
10:30am	Workshop Breakout Session on The Practice of Negotiations, Adaptive Leadership, Design Thinking and Innovation and Public Narratives
12:00pm	Special Performance by Students of SM Foundation
1:00pm	Briefing and Dialogue with Pia Hontiveros, CNN Correspondent in Manila
3:00pm	Sightseeing of Manila: Rizal Park, San Augustin Church, Philippines National Museum, Intramuros, and Fort Santiago

Sunday, June 7

9:00am	Free and Rest Time at Nasugbu Beach Resort
4:00pm	Travel to Manila

Monday, June 8

9:00am	Dialogue with Jaime Zobel de Ayala, Chairman of the Ayala Group
11:00am	Luncheon with Senior Management of Asia Institute of Management
12:30pm	Special Seminar on 'ASEAN Economic Community and Economic Prospects of the Philippines'
2:00pm	Briefing by the Ministry of Foreign Affairs on 'Philippines' Diplomatic Measures on the Issues Concerning the South China Sea'
4:00pm	Dialogue with Honorable Secretary of the Philippine Department of Budget and Management and Former Education Secretary, Florencio Barsana Abad

Tuesday, June 9

9:00am	Guided Tour of the Asian Development Bank

9:30am	Dialogue with Chief Economists and Senior Officials of the Asian Development Bank on 'Green Energy Corridor and Grid Strengthening Projects' and 'Infrastructure Investment, Private Finance and Institutional Investors'
2:00pm	Guided Tour of the Batasang Pambansa, the Philippine House of Congress
3:00pm	Meeting with House Speaker, Feliciano Belmonte, Jr. and Congressmen at Batasang Pambansa
5:00pm	Dinner with the Harvard Club of the Philippines

Wednesday, June 10

10:00am	Meeting with the JG Summit Holdings
1:00pm	Guided Tour and Dialogue with Senior Leaders of the GMA 7 Network
4:00pm	Travel to Guangzhou, China

Thursday, June 11

10:00am	Meeting with YMCA Guangzhou
12:00pm	Meeting with Stars Youth Development Center, an NGO to Improve Rural Area Education in China
2:00pm	Tour of Guangzhou TV Tower - Second Tallest Tower in the World
4-6pm	**Asia Leadership Conference 2015 in Guangzhou** Group 1: Guangzhou University – Design Thinking and Innovation Group 2: Sun Yat-sen University – Entrepreneurship and Intrapreneurship Group 3: Guangzhou No. 2 High School – Leadership Communications Group 4: Guangzhou Experimental High School – Adaptive Leadership Group 5: Guangzhou Guangya High School – Cross-Cultural Communications Group 6: Zhixin High School – Building a Powerful Personal Branding

Hosted Dinner by Lixin Company

Friday, June 12

10:00am	Guided Tour of Tencent Company
10:30am	Dialogue with Senior Leaders of Tencent
1:00pm	Company Tour of Huawei and Meeting with Senior Leaders
3:00pm	Company Tour of DJI Drone Company and Meeting with Senior Leaders
5:00pm	Guided Tour and Dialogue with Senor Leaders of Qianhai Free Trade Zone
6:00pm	Visit to the China-Hong Kong Entrepreneur Academy
7:00pm	Travel to Hong Kong via Bus
9:00pm	Welcome Dinner and Conference Preparation

Saturday, June 13

9:00am – 6:00pm	**Asia Leadership Conference 2015 in Hong Kong at Chinese University of Hong Kong**
9:00am	Registration
9:30am	Opening Remarks by Hungsoo S. Kim, President of ALT
9:35am	Welcoming Speech by Andrew Chi-fai Chan, Head of Shaw College, The Chinese University of Hong Kong
9:40am	Special Talk 1 by Adam Malaty-Uhr (US, HGSE Ed.M.) on 'Developing of a Leader'
9:55am	Special Talk 2 by Katie Mulroy (US, HGSE Ed.M.) on Study Abroad: Promoting Access for All
10:10am	Tea Break and Networking Session
10:30am	Panel Discussion on 'Leadership Attributes for the New Economy,' by Aaron Kleiman (US, HKS MCMPA), Sirin Akaraphan (Thailand, Wharton MBA and HKS MPA), Gregoire Jayot (France, HKS MPA), and Rachel Roberts (US, HGSE Ed.M.), Hany Beshr (Egypt, HKS MCMPA) and Evelien Blom (The Netherlands, HKS MPA) moderated by Marina Chan (Hong Kong, HGSE Ed.M.)
11:30am	Break

11:40am	Workshop Breakout Session A on The Practice of Negotiations, Adaptive Leadership, Design Thinking and Innovation, Public Narratives, Becoming a Leader, and Manager and Leader
1:00pm	Lunch
2:00pm	Workshop Breakout Session B on the Same Topics
3:20pm	Tea Break and Networking Session
3:40pm	Career Mentoring and Professional Development Seminar on Managing LinkedIn, Writing Essay, Career in Legal Profession, Career in Education and Career in Strategy and Management Consulting
5:00pm	Closing Remarks by Hungsoo S. Kim, President of ALT
6:30pm	Dinner at Jumbo Floating Restaurant

Sunday, June 14

| 9:00am | Sightseeing of Hong Kong: Victoria Peak, Tian Tan Buddha, Ngong Ping 360, Po Lin Monastery, Hong Kong Museum of History, Man Po Temple, Ten Thousand Buddhas Monastery, Clock Tower, Tung Choi Street and Wong Tai Sin Street |

Monday, June 15

9:30am	Visit to the Blueprint, Accelerator Program of Swire Property & Dialogue with Senior Management
11:00am	Dialogue with Charles Ng, Associate Director-General of Investment Promotion 2 of the InvestHK, Government Unit Promoting Business from Overseas
2:00pm	Dialogue with Senior Leaders of the Hong Kong Council of Social Service
4:30pm	Dialogue with Ip Kin-Yuen, Member of Education Constituency, Legislative Council of Hong Kong
6:30pm	Mixer with Harvard Club of Hong Kong

Tuesday, June 16

| 10:00am | Meeting with Social Ventures HK at The Good Lab, Co-working Space for Social Enterprises |

11:00am	Meeting with Diamond Cab, a Social Enterprise
2:30pm	Guided Tour of theAsia Miles Company & Dialogue with Stephen Wong, CEO of Asia Miles
4:15pm	Guided Tour of the Cathay Pacific Innovation Center and Presentation by Bidyut Dumra, Director of the Center
7:50pm	Travel to Bangkok, Thailand

Wednesday, June 17

9:00am	Sightseeing of Bangkok: Grand Palace, Wat Phra Kaew, Reclining Buddha, Wat Benchamabophit, Wat Suthat, Bangkok National Museum, and National Museum of Royal Barges

Thursday, June 18

10:00am	Guided Tour of the Stock Exchange of Thailand (SET)
10:30am	Dialogue with Charamporn Jotikasthira, President and CEO of SET
11:30am	Luncheon with Board of Governors and Senior Leaders of SET
1:30pm	Dialogue with Prasarn Trairatvorakul, Governor of the Bank of Thiland
4:00pm	Dialogue with Dr. Mechai Viravidya, Founder of Population Community Development Association
5:30pm	Dialogue with Dr. Kriengsak Chareonwongsak, President of the Institute of Future Studies for Development in Thailand and Chairman of Success Group of Companies

Friday, June 19

10:00am	Dialogue with Narong Chearavanont, Chief Commercial Officer and Chief Merchandize Officer of CP Group
1:00pm	Meeting with Senior Leaders of C-ASEAN
3:30pm	Meeting with the International Labor Organization Thailand on Migrant Worker Issues in Thailand
6:30pm	Dinner and Dialogue with Leaders and Entrepreneurs at HUBBA, Thailand Startup Incubator

Saturday, June 20

9:00am – 1:00pm	**Asia Leadership Conference 2015 in Bangkok with Teach For Thailand**
9:00am	Opening Remarks by Hungsoo S. Kim, President of ALT
9:10am	Workshops on The Practice of Negotiations and Leadership Communications
10:30am	Panel Discussion on the 'New Perspectives on Leadership' by Hungsoo S. Kim (Korea, HKS MPA), Pitichoke Chulapamornsri (Thailand, HKS MPP), and Annika Lawrence (US, HGSE Ed.M.)
2:00pm	Optional Tour to Amphawa Floating Market via Bus
11:30pm	Travel to Seoul, Korea

Sunday, June 21

9:00am	Sightseeing of Seoul Group 1: Myungdong, Gwanghwamun, Gyungbokgung, and Insadong Group 2: Bukchon, Gwangwhamun, Seoul City Hall, and Yongsan
	Group 3: Gangnam, Bongeunsa, Lotte World, and Olympic Park Group 4: Yeouido, National Museum of Korea, War Memorial, and 63 Building
6:00pm	Watching the JUMP Show, Martial Arts Comedy Show

Monday, June 22

9:00am	Free & Rest Time
2:00pm	Meeting with Social Entrepreneurs on the Issues of Creating Shared Values and Corporate Social Responsibilities
5:00pm	Meeting with North Korean Defectors
6:00pm	Special Talk by Casey Lartigue, President of Teach North Korean Refugee

Tuesday, June 23

9:00am	Dialogue with the Chairwoman of the Foreign Affairs and Unification Committee of the National Assembly, Na Gyungwon
10:00am	Dialogue with the Honorable Speaker of the National Assembly, Chung Ui-hwa
11am	Guided Tour of the National Assembly
1:00pm	Guided Tour of Imjingak
2:00pm	Tour of the Odusan Unification Observatory
5:00pm	Dialogue with Senior Leaders of Kim & Chang
5:30pm	Special Lecture by Dr. Park Jin, Senior Advisor of Kim & Chang on 'Geopolitics Surrounding South Korea'
6:30pm	Dinner & Networking Session with Kim & Chang Attoneys

Wednesday, June 24

9:00am	Taekwondo Class
2:30pm	Travel to Ulaan Baatar
7:00pm	Welcome Dinner

Thursday, June 25

9:00am	Press Conference
10:00am	Dialogue with Honorable Prime Minister of Mongolia, Chimed Saikhanbileg
11:00am	Dialogue with Honorable Speaker of the Parliament, Miyeegombyn Enkhbold
12:00pm	Lunch with Women Parliament Members
1:00pm	Guided Tour of the Parliament and Museum
2:30pm	Dialogue with Honorable Minister of Mining Energy, Byanma Jigjid on 'Prospects of Energy Market Development in Mongolia'
4:00pm	Dialogue with Honorable Minister of Environment, Green Development and Tourism, D. Oyunkhorol on 'Government Measure to Promote Tourism Industry and Curbing Environmental Degradation

6:00pm	Dinner with the Harvard Club of Mongolia Hosted by Bishrelt Group

Friday, June 26

9:30am	Dialogue with Senior Executives of the Oyu Tolgoi
11:00am	Dialogue with Batshugar Enkhbayar, Deputy Governor of the Bank of Mongolia
12:00pm	Guided Tour of the State Treasury Exhibition at the Central Bank
1:00pm	Dialogue with Mayor of Ulaan Baatar, Erdeniin Bat-Uul
2:00pm	Luncheon with Ganzorig Ulziibayar, CEO at Golomt Bank
4:00pm	"Be Global" Conference on the '21st Century Education and Skills' to 800 Middle & High School Students of Mongolia - Special Talk 1 by Adam Malaty-Uhr (US, HGSE Ed.M.) on 'Developing of a Leader' - Special Talk 2 by Oyun-Erdene Luvsan (Mongolia, HKS MCMPA) on 'Becoming an Effective Change Agent' - Special Talk 3 by Annika Lawrence (US, HGSE Ed.M.) on 'Overcoming Adversities' - Special Talk 4 by Hungsoo S. Kim (Korea, HKS MPA) on 'Leadership is about Thinking and Taking Actions'
7:00pm	Dinner Hosted by Executive Excellence Center at Galaxy tower
8:00pm	Special Seminar on 'Opportunities and Challenges to Doing Business in Mongolia' by Mongolia Business Database

Saturday, June 27

9-6pm	**Asia Leadership Conference 2015 in Ulaan Baatar**
8:30am	Registration
9:00am	Opening Remarks by Hungsoo S. Kim, President of ALT
9:10am	Special Talk on 'Developing of a Leader' by Adam Malaty-Uhr (US, HGSE Ed.M.)

9:30am	Forum Discussion on 'From Good Intention to Leading Social Change' by Anna Stansbury (Great Britain, HKS MPP), Greg Manne (US, HGSE Ed.M.), Annika Lawrence (US, HGSE, Ed.M.), Clare Carlo (US, Fletcher MALD), Pitichoke Chulapamornsri (Thailand, HKS MPA), and Simon Muller (Germany, HKS MPA)
11:00am	Tea Break & Networking Session
11:20am	Workshop Breakout Session 1
12:40pm	Lunch
1:20pm	Workshop Breakout Session 2
2:40pm	Tea Break & Networking Session
3:00pm	Career Mentoring Session
4:20pm	Break
4:40pm	Professional Skills Development Session
6:00pm	Closing Remarks by Hungsoo S. Kim, President of ALT
7:00pm	Gala Dinner with Mongolian Thought Leaders

Sunday, June 28

9:00am	Travel to Terelj Steppe
11:00am	Hiking & Horse Riding
9:00pm	Overnight Stay at Ger

Monday, June 29

9:00am	Travel to Ulaan Baatar
1:30pm	Dialogue with Honorable Minister of Road Transportation, Amarjargal Gansukh
3:00pm	Sightseeing of Ulaan Baatar: National Museum, Winter Palace of Bogd Khan and Choijin Lama Temple
7:00pm	Shopping at Gobi Cashmere Factory
8:00pm	Appreciation & Farewell Dinner

Tuesday, June 30

	Depart for Boston

| Appendix II |

List of Trekkers and Fellows

• • ●

Asia Leadership Trek 2015

Abdulaziz Said, *American*
MPP, Harvard Kennedy School of Government

Adauto Modesto Junior, *Brazilian*
MPP, Harvard Kennedy School of Government

Ahava Silkey-Jones, *American*
Ed.M., Harvard Graduate School of Education

Alanna Hughes, *American*
MPA, Harvard Kennedy School of Government
MBA, MIT Sloan School of Management

Alison Flint, *American*
MPP, Harvard Kennedy School of Government

Aviva Feuerstein, *American*
MPP, Harvard Kennedy School of Government

Bryant Renaud, *American*
MPP, Harvard Kennedy School of Government

Caitlin Callahan, *American*
MPP, Harvard Kennedy School of Government

Cathy Guo, *Chinese*
MPP, Harvard Kennedy School of Government

Cedrick Jones, *American*
BA, Elmhurst College

Clara Carolina de Sa, *Brazilian*
LLB, Catholic University Center

Claude Al Tabar, *Lebanese*
MPA/ID, Harvard Kennedy School of Government

David Rose, *American*
MPP, Harvard Kennedy School of Government
MBA, Harvard Business School

Elizabeth Peyton, *American*
MALD, Tufts Fletcher School of Law and Diplomacy

Emily Kunz, *American*
MA, Tufts Fletcher School of Law and Diplomacy

Fayrouz Saad, *American*
MPA, Harvard Kennedy School of Government

Francesca Ioffreda, *American*

MPP, Harvard Kennedy School of Government

MBA, Harvard Business School

Hungsoo S. Kim, *Korean*

President, Center for Asia Leadership Initiatives

MPA, Harvard Kennedy School of Government

Javier Fuentes, *Chilean*

MPA, Harvard Kennedy School of Government

MBA, MIT Sloan School of Management

Jiro Yoshino, *Japanese*

MPA, Harvard Kennedy School of Government

Joel Burns, *American*

MPA, Harvard Kennedy School of Government

Joel Smoot, *American*

MPP, Harvard Kennedy School of Government

Jooyeon June Koo, *American*

MPP, Harvard Kennedy School of Government

Joseph Sakran, *American*

MPA, Harvard Kennedy School of Government

Rafael Rivera, *Mexican*

MPA/ID, Harvard Kennedy School of Government

MBA, Harvard Business School

Kaihan Yang, *Chinese*
Ph.D., University of Derby

Katherine Sooah Cho, *American*
MPP, Harvard Kennedy School of Government
MBA, Harvard Business School

Nawal Lyana Binti Nafiz, *Malaysian*
ACCA, Sunway College

Neha Sharma, *Indian*
MPA, Harvard Kennedy School of Government

Parul Batra, *Indian*
MBA, MIT Sloan School of Management

Rachel Mason, *American*
Ed.M., Harvard Graduate School of Education

Raghav Goel, *Indian*
MBA, MIT Sloan School of Management

Rajat Sethi, *Indian*
MPA, Harvard Kennedy School of Government
MBA, MIT Sloan School of Management

Rohit Sudarshan, *American*
MALD, Tufts Fletcher School of Law and Diplomacy

Santhi Suppiah, *Malaysian*
Senior Lecturer, Sunway College

Shruthi Saravanan, *Indian*
Ed.M., Harvard Graduate School of Education

Simon Malian, *Australian*
MA, Harvard Graduate School of Arts and Sciences

Soojin Park, *Korean*
BA, Duke University

Susanne Schwarz, *German*
MPP, Harvard Kennedy School of Government

Tan Li Jean, *Malaysian*
BSc, Sunway University

Taniel Chan, *American*
MPP, Harvard Kennedy School of Government
MBA, Harvard Business School

Vincent Lampone, *American*
MPA, Harvard Kennedy School of Government

Vivian Yuhang Wang, *Chinese*
MBA, Harvard Business School

● ● ●

Korea and Mongolia Leadership Trek

Anji Sauve Clubb, *American*
MDes, Harvard Graduate School of Design

Oyunerdene Luvsannamsrai, *Mongolian*
MPA, Harvard Kennedy School of Government

Khongorzul Bat-Ireedui, *Mongolian*
MALD, Tufts Fletcher School of Law and Diplomacy

Hungsoo S. Kim, *Korean*
President, Center for Asia Leadership Initiatives
MPA, Harvard Kennedy School of Government

John Lim, *Canadian/Filipino*
Yonsei/Fletcher, Harvard Extension School

Jiro Yoshino, *Japanese*
MPA, Harvard Kennedy School of Government
Paola Cordovez, *Ecuadorean*
MPP, Harvard Kennedy School of Government

Rabi' Sweidan, *French/Lebanese*
MPA, Harvard Kennedy School of Government

Filipe Correa Nasser Silva, *Brazilian*
MPA, Harvard Kennedy School of Government

Chris Stavrianou, *Canadian/Greek*
MPA, Harvard Kennedy School of Government

Santiago Caviedes, *Ecuadorean*
MPA, Harvard Kennedy School of Government

David Klausner *American*
MPP, Harvard Kennedy School of Government

Soojin Park, *Korean*
BA, Duke University

Nagi Otgonshar, *Mongolian*
MBA, Harvard Business School

● ● ●

Asia Leadership Trek V

Aaron Kleiman, *American*
MPA, Harvard Kennedy School of Government

Adam Malaty-Uhr, *American*
Ed.M., Harvard Graduate School of Education

Amy Choi, *Korean*
BA, Yonsei University

Anna Stansbury, *British*
MPP, Harvard Kennedy School of Government

Annie Yu Kleiman, *American*
MALD, Tufts Fletcher School of Law and Diplomacy

Annika Lawrence, *Jamaican/American*
Ed.M., Harvard Graduate School of Education

Caitlin Hartman, *American*
MPP, Harvard Kennedy School of Government

Chaitanya Kansal, *Indian*
BTech, Indian Institute of Technology Patna

Clare Claro, *American*
MALD, Tufts Fletcher School of Law and Diplomacy

Evelien Blom, *Dutch*
MPA, Harvard Kennedy School of Government

Greg Manne, *American*
Ed.M., Harvard Graduate School of Education

Gregoire Jayot, *French*
MPA, Harvard Kennedy School of Government

Hany Beshr, *Egyptian*
MPA, Harvard Kennedy School of Government

Jeff Chen, *Hongkonger*
BSc, Hong Kong University of Science & Technology

Jiro Yoshino, *Japanese*
MPA, Harvard Kennedy School of Government

John Lim, *Canadian/Filipino*
Yonsei/Fletcher, Harvard Extension School

Katie Mulroy, *American*
Ed.M., Harvard Graduate School of Education

Kevin Tan, *Singaporean*
MPP, Harvard Kennedy School of Government

Khongorzul Bat-Ireedui, *Mongolian*
MALD, Tufts Fletcher School of Law and Diplomacy

Lisa Marie Gomez, *American*
MPA, Harvard Kennedy School of Government

Mahfuzul Islam, *American*
MA, Harvard Graduate School of Arts and Sciences

Marina Chan, *Hongkonger*
Ed.M., Harvard Graduate School of Education

Masoomeh Khandan, *Iranian*
MPA/ID, Harvard Kennedy School of Government

Nourhan Beshr, *Egyptian*
BA, German University in Cairo

Ofir Zigelman, *Israeli*
MPA, Harvard Kennedy School of Government

Oyunerdene Luvsannamsrai, *Mongolian*
MPA, Harvard Kennedy School of Government

Pitichoke Chulapamornsri, *American*
MPP, Harvard Kennedy School of Government

Rachel Roberts, *American*
Ed.M., Harvard Graduate School of Education

Simon Mueller, *German*
MPA, Harvard Kennedy School of Government

Sirin Akaraphan, *Thai*
MPA, Harvard Kennedy School of Government
MBA, The Wharton School, University of Pennsylvania

Taeko Kohara, *Japanese*
MALD, Tufts Fletcher School of Law and Diplomacy

Ting Chen, *American*
BS, Syracuse University

Yingxin Wang, *Chinese*
AM in RSEA, Harvard Graduate School of Arts and Sciences

Zolbayar Jargalsaikhan, *Mongolian*
BA, Peking University

• • •

Asia Leadership Fellowship Spring 2015

Jeremy Blaney, *American*
MALD, Tufts Fletcher School of Law and Diplomacy

John Lim, *Canadian/Filipino*
Yonsei/Fletcher, Harvard Extension School

Sean Glazebrook, *American*
Ed.M., Harvard Graduate School of Education

Kathy Qu, *Canadian*
Ed.M., Harvard Graduate School of Education
BA, Princeton University

Mehjabeen Zameer, *Pakistani*
Ed.M., Harvard Graduate School of Education

Chelsey Evans, *American*
MALD, Tufts Fletcher School of Law and Diplomacy

Shashank Shukla, *Indian*
MPA, Harvard Kennedy School of Government

Dara Fisher, *American*
Ed.D., Harvard Graduate School of Education
S.M., Massachusetts Institute of Technology

● ● ●

Asia Leadership Fellowship Summer 2015

Aaron Kleinman, *American*
MPA, Harvard Kennedy School of Government

Adam Malaty-Uhr, *American*
Ed.D., Harvard Graduate School of Education

Evelyn Peiqi Ooi Widjaja, *Malaysian*
Ed.M., Harvard Graduate School of Education

Faton Limani, *Kosovan*
MPA, Harvard Kennedy School of Government

Hungsoo S. Kim, *Korean*
President, Center for Asia Leadership Initiatives
MPA, Harvard Kennedy School of Government

Jaye Buchbinder, *American*
MSE, Stanford University

John Lee, *American*
MPA, Harvard Kennedy School of Government

John Lim, *Canadian/Filipino*
Yonsei/Fletcher, Harvard Extension School

Martin Attiq, *American*
MSx, Stanford Graduate School of Business

Rachel Roberts, *American*
Ed.M., Harvard Graduate School of Education

| Appendix III |

List of Conference Topics

●●●

Asia Leadership Conference

Workshop Topics

1. Addressing Cognitive Biases in Decision Making
2. Adaptive Leadership
3. Art of Communication
4. Authentic Leadership
5. Becoming a Better Decision Maker
6. Better Together: Empowering Effective Collaboration between Men and Women
7. Building a Public Narrative
8. Building Bridges through Inter-Cultural and Ethnic Dialogue
9. Campaigns 101: How to Run and Manage a Campaign
10. Creating and Claiming Value in Negotiations
11. Creating Inclusive Workplaces–Targeting and Minimizing Conflict
12. Creating Shared Value
13. Cross-Cultural Communication: Embracing Others and

40. Social Entrepreneurship: From Idea to Realization
41. The Art of Effective Advocacy
42. The Reflective Leader
43. Transformational Leadership
44. Using Stories to Mobilize Change
45. Women and Leadership

Career Mentoring Topics

1. Applying to US Universities: General
2. Applying to US Universities: Finding and Choosing the Right Program
3. Applying to US Universities: MBA, MPA or JD Programs
4. Career in Academics, Research and Think Tanks
5. Career in Advocacy and Campaigning
6. Career in Education
7. Career in Engineering-General
8. Career in Finance & Banking
9. Career in Foreign Service
10. Career in International Development & Aid
11. Career in Legal
12. Career in Marketing
13. Career in Management Consulting
14. Career in Medicine & Health
15. Career in Nonprofit
16. Career in Politics
17. Career in Social Entrepreneurship
18. Career in Sports

19. Leadership Coaching
20. ech Start-ups

Professional Development Topics

1. All About Publishing Your Own Book
2. Building a Personal Branding
3. Building Resume
4. Creative Writing
5. Developing a Powerful and Persuasive Voice
6. Dressing for Success
7. Essential Presentation Skills
8. Giving an Elevator Pitch
9. Giving an Impromptu Speech
10. Interviewing Skills: Jobs
11. Interviewing Skills: Media
12. Job Search Efforts in the Times of Transition
13. Managing Your Online Presence: LinkedIn
14. Managing Effective Small Talks
15. Networking and Building Contacts
16. Social Media–How to Make or Break Your Life
17. Transitioning from School to Work or Vice-Versa
18. Writing a Business Plan
19. Writing a Great Op-ed
20. Writing a News Article
21. Writing a Powerful Speech
22. Writing a Statement of Purpose
23. Writing Good Recommendation Letters

| Appendix IV |
List of Contributors

● ● ●

Introduction

Hungsoo S. Kim, *Korean*
President, Center for Asia Leadership Initiatives
MPA, Harvard Kennedy School of Government

● ● ●

Asia Leadership Trek IV

Vivian Yuhang Wang, *Chinese*
MBA, Harvard Business School

Alanna Hughes, *American*
MPA, Harvard Kennedy School of Government
MBA, MIT Sloan School of Management

Greg Manne, *American*
Ed.M., Harvard Graduate School of Education

Parul Batra, *Indian*
MBA, MIT Sloan School of Management

Bryant Renaud, *American*
MPP, Harvard Kennedy School of Government

Rachel Mason, *American*
Ed.M., Harvard Graduate School of Education

●●●

Asia Leadership Fellowship 2014

Evelyn Peiqi Ooi Widjaja, *Malaysian*
Ed.M., Harvard Graduate School of Education

Jaye Buchbinder, *American*
MSE, Stanford University

Eugene B. Kogan, *American*
Teaching Scholar, Harvard Kennedy School of Government

John Lim, *Canadian/Filipino*
Yonsei/Fletcher, Harvard Extension School

www.ingramcontent.com/pod-product-compliance
Lightning Source LLC
Chambersburg PA
CBHW051552250726
48653CB00004BA/1120

On Being Progressive:
A Guide to Walking the Path

Author: Richard Rossi (AI assisted)

Dedicated to those who have taught me so much.

August, 2024